Practical Astral Projection

by

YRAM

SAMUEL WEISER INC.
New York
1969

Kessinger Publishing's Rare Reprints
Thousands of Scarce and Hard-to-Find Books!

Contents

7

PART TWO

SOME RELATIONSHIPS BETWEEN MAN AND THE UNIVERSE

Foreword

THE present work takes the place of the three volumes which were originally intended to appear on this subject. Since the publication of my work *Aimez-vous les uns les autres* I decided that further information would in no way help to convince sceptics steeped in the mire of self-satisfaction.

It seems to me that to describe the results of certain experiments, to explain in a logical manner certain problems which concern our future life, will be enough to lead those who wish to win free of the superstitions and errors of the present life, to the study with which this book is concerned.

We shall leave the problem of suffering to others who are at the beginning of their study of life. For ourselves, who do not think of the worldly life as being of great import, we shall try, on the contrary, to realize a finer existence, a fuller and freer consciousness, free as much as possible of all inconveniences which are but obstacles to the peace we are seeking.

All treatises on morality can be reduced to a scheme rationally based upon our motives for performing any particular act or acts. When there exists a lack of interest, then logic and common sense are no longer enough for us. An absolute, unshakable faith in the fundamental principles of our being is alone capable of giving our motives the necessary impetus for putting them into practice.

The experimental knowledge of a state of life existing outside the physical world gives our faith an added strength now unknown for several centuries.

I am not exaggerating in claiming that the propagation of this particular knowledge will cause humanity to enter into a new evolutionary period.

For the layman there will always exist honest and dishonest people. The Initiate, on the other hand, whose vision penetrates into another dimension, sees this evolutionary wave in terms of progressive states of consciousness, and he perceives a mass of human beings striding boldly into the higher regions of the Eternal Substance. Those who accomplish this feat will return no more. Free from the need of once more taking up a physical body they will gladly make room for others less advanced.

What is more, a thousand years hence, the ignoramus of that period will cry out like his present-day prototype, that all efforts made to improve the lot of the individual are useless, because in those days suffering and chaos will still reign, up to a certain point, over the inhabitants of this earth.

PART ONE

THE EXPERIMENTAL BASES OF THE SCIENTIFIC, PHILOSOPHIC, AND RELIGIOUS UNITY OF OPINIONS AND BELIEFS

CHAPTER I

A NEW SCIENTIFIC BASIS FOR PROGRESS

AMONG the many aspects of modern knowledge the most difficult matter upon which to form a rational opinion is one's own existence. This ignorance brings with it a mass of fallacies in all other aspects of life. Social progress, in the minds of many persons, represents the only reality, and the modern aim seems to consist in being able to imagine a state where everyone will be able to do as he pleases.

This Utopian conception, carefully fed by the various interested parties, has developed a crystallization in modern thought. Science, Religion, and Philosophy are marking time, quite unconscious of the fact that they are doing so. A great deal is being written, far less being thought. Therefore, as soon as a work treats of questions which call for prolonged thinking on the part of the reader, it is hastily put away at the bottom of a drawer.

The world of to-day is always in a hurry. Each individual wants to see immediate results, without worrying in the least as to the causes which bring them about.

Yet, never within the history of our race has the

time been more propitious for the reform of our
ideas, to a greater and speedier progress, all leading
towards social harmony and happiness.

From what source shall we take the Mother Idea,
origin of all future changes? What is the new
element whose energy will impregnate our knowledge with its radio-active potentialities? On what
basis are we to stand in order to balance our various
opinions and beliefs, with a healthy, clearly conceived reality?

So far as hypotheses are concerned we are
burdened with too many already! The Great War
of 1914 upset many castles in the air which had
been built upon the illusion of goodwill. Religions
are no longer competent to deal with their task.
The majority of these are lacking in the most rudimentary common sense. So far as the theories of
so-called scientific philosophies are concerned these
would drag us back to the era of our cave-dwelling
ancestors by exalting the conception of our animal
origin.

Logic pure and simple is no longer enough.
Despite the presumed advancement of our civilization, modern thought is lacking in food. The bases
of true morality are misconceived, and the human
soul wanders aimlessly in the void of illusion and
chimeric hopes.

The great problem which has always been present
before the human being is that of survival. If we
were able to know exactly what would happen to
us after death, if we could only know in an absolutely
certain manner if it is possible to live, to see, to feel,
think, and understand in another state of being
with the same ease as we have done these on earth,

what enormous strides could be made in our evolution.

Without the least exaggeration we could claim that this knowledge would be the greatest revolution which has ever been accomplished in all the realms of our activity. And if this knowledge can bring about some relief of human suffering, then one may definitely claim that the knowledge of this secular enigma is one of the greatest benefits that one could give to humanity.

This fact, this faith through personal experience, this understanding, is being brought within your reach by means of the present work.

It is not necessary that you should have faith. I am not approaching you as a missionary charged with the propagation of a new idea. I am simply putting forward the results I have personally obtained, saying: "There is nothing in the least mysterious in what I have done. This is the way in which I have set about the matter; all you have to do is to reproduce the experiment under the same conditions and you will obtain the same results."

It is obvious that, at first glance, this claim is unbelievable. To the average mind it will seem that the unveiling of such an important mystery, without any possible doubt, could be only a dream brought about by too much delving into mystical and occult books during the silent hours of the night. Think of the many mightier brains that have been harnessed to the great problem without being able to find its solution! And is it not obvious that were it easy for the first-comer to penetrate with such ease the mystery of planes, hitherto believed to be inaccessible, this secret would be popular knowledge? Were it all so easy, humanity would not have had to wait centuries and centuries to penetrate behind the veil and to understand a mystery in the name of which so many human beings have been massacred—for the salvation of their souls!

Were it not that I have solved the enigma myself, I would certainly make the same remarks and probably add: "The poor fellow must have suffered from brain fever in his youth and is showing signs of the after-effects of that disease."

No doubt my readers will be more polite, and they will probably conclude that auto-suggestion or hallucinations have brought about some special psychosis in my brain, and that I would do well to consult a specialist in the cure of such afflictions.

However pertinent these suggestions may seem, they will not alter the experience in the least degree. I have myself gone over all the arguments that any-one could put forward, gone deeply into the possibility that I might be a pathological case. For years I compared the results of my experiments with all the traditional teachings which came before me. I analysed the essential characteristics of all the different religions and philosophies, I dissected the nature of man according to the most up-to-date scientific knowledge, and found no flagrant contradictions with my experimental observations.

Besides, there is one salient fact which stands out in relation to the whole of human knowledge; that is, that our knowledge follows a natural process of development at all times. In order that the fruit of wisdom may be plucked we must await its ripening. Each stage in human knowledge is the result of causes initiated, perhaps, thousands of years prior to their manifestation.

And, when the fruit of wisdom is ripe, the personality of the individual who has the luck to find it is of little import. His most obvious duty is to share this treasure with others, irrespective of the reception which falls to his lot.

CHAPTER II

THE best way in which the problem of survival could be solved would be to die, in order to observe the details of the phenomenon in a precise manner. This is, from a practical point of view, impossible, the more so if we do not happen to believe in spirits. A more subtle solution is required. Whilst studying the different traditional systems and philosophies one notices, among their symbolism, ideas concerning the possibilities of separating the human being into two distinct parts, without his having to undergo too much discomfort.

The mesmerists, and especially Hector Durville,[1] have studied this phenomenon by experiment on willing subjects and obtained most satisfactory results.

For the sceptic, though, this kind of experiment gives rise to too many difficulties. But suppose we could, each one of us, voluntarily put ourselves into the same condition, could leave our bodies just as we go through our front door, without for one second losing full control of all our conscious faculties; that would be truly interesting! No

[1] *Vide* Hector Durville : *Le Fantôme des vivants.*

more mysteries or complications of any sort. We would merely change our dimension.

Knowledge so obtained is of more use than that obtained by dying. When the body is disorganized by disease the mind is anxious and our faculties are not in the best state to examine the process of separation between body and soul.

To be capable of renewing this experience of disembodiment at will, in full possession of all one's powers, of all one's mental clarity, without trouble of any kind, is, in my opinion, superior to final separation. Such are the conditions which I have observed during the fourteen years since I succeeded in my first experiment. Needless to say, I have had plenty of time to become used to the finer state and to study it in detail. Moreover, I soon became sated with ordinary phenomena. To pass through stone walls, to visit friends, to roam freely in space simply for the sake of enjoying this extraordinary state, are games of which one soon wearies. Human consciousness is more greedy, it seeks to travel further; this new dimension is not enough to satisfy it, it seeks to penetrate into another form of the cosmic organization.

Truly the human being is insatiable and so it happened that travelling from dimension to dimension, I was not satisfied until I had attained that almost indescribable state when one is no more than a "unity-multiplicity" with the higher energy of nature. Of course, there are many obstacles in the way, but these are within one's means to overcome. It took me exactly twelve years to develop my consciousness and to penetrate with it to the extreme boundary of our universe. It became necessary for me to carry out a whole series of operations on my psychological being. These, though, mostly took place in so gentle a manner as to be imperceptible. With each stage, which might well be compared to a new death, because its development takes from us some part of our affections, we must adapt ourselves to a new mental regimen. This must go on until the last renunciation comes, when we take the great decisive leap into the unknown, and the conscious being loses the last vestige of his personality. Yet I claim that this evolution lies within the grasp of everyone who takes the trouble to experiment.[1]

Taking into consideration the period over which these experiments were carried out, the mass of evidence which I gathered in other dimensions of space, I am in a position to give absolutely precise details on the question of existence outside one's physical form.

My task is all the more difficult when one considers the almost total ignorance of these matters on the part of the general public. A widespread knowledge of such feats is even dangerous. To place an experience of such major importance within the reach of everyone is equivalent to handing over the secret of new forms of energy which can be used for evil. I spent a long time meditating on this problem and these are the results of my search. From experience I have realized that evil can only touch those who are open to it, owing to the inherent evil in their own natures. Furthermore, the efforts which have to be put forth call for a certain psychological and physical balance from which evil is

---

[1] This strange evolutionary process is described in a further volume by the author : *L'Evolution dans les mondes supérieurs.*

excluded.   Lastly, if, by some exceptional means, an evil-doer were to arrive at some results, he would quickly become the victim of his own nature; so I shall not give too exact information in this work.

I hope that my readers will not hold this against me, and will understand the motive which causes me to act thus.   As in all fields of work, there are certain "tricks of the trade" which only come with practice. In general these are of no great importance, and there is enough in this book to guide anyone in such a way that he or she will be able to succeed alone.

Besides, anything that has been omitted is only an open secret, well enough known to many occultists. In the present work we are not concerned with occultism nor with mysterious or sectarian operations of magic.   The work which has to be undertaken in order to penetrate consciously into the fourth dimension is within the reach of all.   In saying this, I am not pretending that effort is unnecessary.   It is quite easy for anyone to read a newspaper, provided that he, or she, has learned the language in which it is printed.

There are still far too many unknown quantities to be discovered before the experience can be defined with the same exactitude as a chemical analysis.   For the moment it is enough that we can obtain results from what we know, and that these results improve progressively with practice.   "Time" is the only factor which cannot be limited.   This time-element is reduced in proportion to the concentrated intensity with which the student sets about his task.   For instance, the student who will put his whole being into this work, without reservation of any kind, who will sacrifice on its altar his whole wealth, his friendship, his dearest thoughts, his life, even, if that becomes necessary, will reach the goal far quicker than another student who retains in the depths of his heart some selfish tendencies.

It must be thoroughly realized that in this phenomenon of dissociation between the physical and other aspects of the human being, it is not appearances which count, but the real work which has been done, the intimate, unseen efforts made by the human "I" to free itself from its attachments to the crude forms of the objective life, and to its earthly ties.

In this state hypocrisy disappears and the soul stands naked. Better to attempt nothing than to undertake the study of these phenomena with any hidden motive of self-interest.

.   .   .   .

The essential conditions required to bring this experiment to a successful issue are of three kinds: physical, psychological, and psychical.

The physical qualities can easily be summed up in the words "good health." People with heart trouble should avoid experimenting.

If one is timid, subject to nervous troubles, it is necessary, before attempting anything, to begin by treating oneself and obtaining calm. The nervo-lymphatic temperament seems to be the best, as people who possess it have the greatest self-mastery.

Excess of any kind must be avoided. Eat in

wise moderation, avoiding highly alcoholic drinks. (This includes strong spirits like whisky, brandy, gin, etc., but allows a moderation of wine and beer, though the latter is not so good.) A careful eye must be kept on the functioning of the organism, and the temperature and heart-beat, etc., should be noted every day. Adapt the psychical exercises in accordance with this examination.

The training of the psychological being is of particular importance. We must always keep in mind the nature of the work to be carried out. This is not a matter of trying an experiment for after-dinner amusement. It is essential to realize the serious nature of the undertaking. In olden times the neophyte was prepared for this mystery by years of arduous training and, even then, all were not successful. Now, try to imagine the brutal transition, the radical change, which you will experience on the day when you find yourself separated in two parts yet in full possession of all your conscious faculties. I must, as in duty bound, warn you that the difference between the reality and the illusions which are taught us by present-day civilization, brings about an extremely violent reaction. It is for this reason that the first of our principles is to be in good health, without any illness or other organic trouble.

At first a peaceful life is necessary. We must avoid worry and bother or, at any rate, not attach any importance to them. Both meditation and prayer are helps towards obtaining this result. These efforts will have an effect on the type of thought in which we indulge, or our desires and motives for any particular act. The shortest way is to choose a noble ideal and to make it the central point round which will shine all thoughts, desires and motives for action. This noble ideal must be your goal; for this alone you should work, and upon it you should concentrate all that is best in you.

Why should this central motive, in which you must concentrate your thoughts, be noble and generous? Because the whole world follows an opposite ideal, namely, that of living as comfortably as possible without considering others at all. This is the ideal of the brute, born of the slime of life. It is the rudimentary state of personal consciousness acquired by the living cells. It is the instinct of self-preservation, it is life which develops according to the law of the strongest and best organized. If you wish to succeed in the exploration of other worlds, without danger, this law must become your servant. It is the first dragon you must conquer, and which will allow you to penetrate into its secrets when it has been mastered.

In order to reach this goal there are two paths. The choice depends on your character, your temperament, your general tendencies, and will-power. The first path consists of overcoming the egotistical tendencies by exercising moderation, by crushing the lower instincts, by giving free rein to generous and noble motives, desires and thoughts. It is the way of moral perfection known to everybody.

The second path is far quicker, but also more painful. It is the way of conscious sacrifice. In this case the suffering entailed is more violent in proportion to the nature and quantity of the elemental nature which has to be driven out. For centuries we have been developing certain kinds of

"energies" which live at our expense. We feed
from our vitality a mass of beings, embryos of life,
which we have attracted by our manner of thinking
and acting, and we must expect a reaction on their
part. One of the favourite methods of these
entities is to inspire in their father a deep disgust, a
moral lassitude, a profound inertia. Not only does
the student see the black side of things, but he may
even go so far as to commit suicide in an access of
despair.

The best thing in such a case is gentleness. We
must avoid being obstinate so far as recalcitrant
tendencies are concerned. Patience is now the
quality which must come into its own. To put all the
ill-will possible into the act of giving way to an
imperfection is a principle of inertia which works
excellently. If, at the same time, we are busily
developing the higher qualities towards which we
feel drawn, the others will die through lack of
nourishment. Last of all, remember that a higher
Love-Principle, chosen as an Ideal, forwards the
work to an incredible degree, and with a minimum
of effort.

Psychism being the order of the day, everyone
knows its methods. The essential points for study
are: The power to concentrate one's thoughts on a
single object without being distracted by outside
stimuli; the practice of rhythmic breathing; nervous
and muscular relaxation; and finally, the ability to
suspend thought completely. This last exercise,
called "withdrawal" by some, and "going into the
silence" by others, sums up the waiting period
necessary before any phenomenon dealing with the
fourth dimension can be expected.

It is not necessary to attain a complete mastery of all these exercises. The practice of self-projection helps to simplify them, and soon they can be dispensed with. All of which goes to show the stupidity of the treatises on magic which consider their formulæ to be axioms.

At all events, whatever your aim may be, remember that the experimental conditions which I am giving represent a minimum of effort, if you want to keep your mental balance. Insanity, congestion, paralysis, the rupture of a blood-vessel, death, are but a few of the dangers that lie in wait for the careless.

Despite the fact that there are no rules without exceptions, I do not suggest that you go forward on this adventure without preparation, because some lack of balance is almost certain. If you neglect psychical training you will not obtain stable phenomena; you will not know how to control them and will risk falling into an unhealthy mysticism. If you neglect the psychological training, it is even worse. You are then heading for an unbalanced mental state owing to the encroachment of lower forces to which you will one day fall a fatal victim.

CHAPTER III

In order to understand what follows, it will be useful if I now give some general observations on several years of study.

These worlds upon which so many hypotheses have been built, these universes which have excited human imagination to the highest pitch, surpass, in their simplicity, anything that man could invent in the way of the marvellous and the complex.

The invisible universe is formless. It reduces itself to an atmosphere impregnated with energy, under a variable pressure.

The Human Being is formless and is also but an electric atmosphere endowed with oscillating energy.

The only difference existing between man and the universe is that collection of psychological factors, represented by consciousness. In the invisible world, a human being is a conscious thought, endowed with an active will. The perception of cause and effect takes place by the help of corresponding sensations in a unit of time. The relation between these two states of being represented by man and the universe is only a question of harmony.

When he leaves his material form, the human being does not take away with him any one action more than another. He only retains the harmonies, the expressions and the rhythm of his experiences on earth. But this is sufficient to attract him and keep him prisoner in a medium where he will be able to put into action his habitual affections.

These harmonious vibrations between the oscillating matter of the subtler worlds and the matter which our consciousness uses for its expression, are translated in the form of innumerable attracting shades which enable us to discern the causes and effects to which they are bound.

The substance of which our universe is made varies from a state of extreme density, which may be designated as "matter," to that radio-active essence to which we give the name of "force." The state which we call "matter" is energy curbed by time and space into a minimum of activity. That which we term "force" is a maximum of instantaneous activity. The steps between these two extremes of the cosmic ladder are numberless, and it is easy to imagine the infinite quantity of individual states which must compose it.

On the "matter" side, a centralizing, centripetal force is dominant. On the "force" side the centrifugal current finds its maximum activity. The evolution of the human being then becomes a simple matter, agreeing in all respects with ancient traditions.

The purpose is to establish in oneself the necessary harmonies to vibrate in agreement with the "force" aspect of matter, and in this way avoid the attraction of the planetary system where all other kinds of attraction would hold us back.

One should be in possession of an absolutely

healthy mind, backed up by sound common sense. In fact, the experience calls for observations which are free from suggestions of all kinds.

Should one remain egotistical the evil would not be so much in this natural attraction, which is essential to the manifestation of primitive life, but rather in the "quality" of the attractions of which one remains a prisoner.

This mechanism gives us the key to altruistic love, a state extolled by all the great thinkers of humanity. By detaching the human being from his lower tendencies, by suppressing his harmonies with the forms of the universal matter, in teaching him to live in a world of higher principles, he becomes accustomed to the handling of the formidable energy to which he is about to have access. I have myself used this method in order to attain unity with the cosmic consciousness and, however unbelievable it may seem at first sight, the results are in absolute harmony with the constitution of our universe.

The matter of the other worlds appears to our observation as an atmosphere of density, luminosity, and of variable vibrationary reactions. Supposing that we are experimenting with a double, composed of a matter of medium density, the following are the characteristics which will be noticed and the sensations which will be experienced.

The field of energy in which pure energy has its being is perceived by an increase or diminution of the centrifugal pull.

In order to maintain a perfect equilibrium in all the degrees of the ether, all attractions must be left behind, in order to reduce the series of vibrations used by the consciousness to its simplest expression.

Until this result is obtained, which represents the goal of human evolution, one notices, in the visible worlds, the existence of a field of energy particularly favourable to the attractions, affinities, and sympathies of the moment.

The quality, the vibratory rhythm of our oscillations, is balanced by a corresponding radio-active condition, and automatically places each human being in matter whose density decides the possibilities which are within his reach.

The power of action within the invisible worlds is therefore limited by the quality, the nature, and the degree of concentration of the harmonious conditions, registered by the consciousness.

By directing these harmonious conditions towards a cosmic unity; that is to say, by referring one's motives for action, thoughts, desires, and affections, to a high ideal, one reaches the domain of the centrifugal force. With a minimum expenditure of energy, we are given access to far greater powers, and in much less time.

On the other hand, by becoming attached to lower pleasures; by concentrating one's life, one's nearest and dearest affections, on the apparent qualities of matter in their attractive but temporary form, one narrows down one's field of action into a state of being where time increases in volume.

The substance of these vast moving waves has the appearance of an atmosphere which varies from the deepest darkness, passing through all the intermediary shades of grey, to radiant clarity. One sees nothing above, beneath, to the right, or to the left.

In descending towards matter, the negative

aspect of energy, the grey atmosphere becomes duller and darker. One experiences the sensation of a substance which becomes steadily thicker. This increase in density is irksome to bear, and it is with difficulty that one can move about in it. The impressions which are received follow the same gradations. We experience the illusion of being oppressed, of breathing with difficulty. A general *malaise* invades us, the consciousness becomes worried and soon the impression becomes definitely painful. In these dark states one sees phosphorescent points which move about in all directions.

When we go towards the positive side of energy, i.e. the negative side of matter, the opacity diminishes. We come into a sort of grey mist, like a cloudy sky. As we rise, the mist becomes thinner, and soon its place is taken by a luminous clarity. A blaze of light, like that of the sun at midday, lights up the atmosphere. Watching carefully, we notice on all sides an equal intensity, showing that this light is produced by the progressive activity in the atoms.

The corresponding sensations are: a gentle warmth which pervades the body we are using; a feeling of exceptional well-being suffusing all its molecules; consciousness itself experiences an increasing happiness. It allows itself to drift into a sweet quietude, into an ever-deepening state of peace. It is filled with a more vibrant, more joyous confidence. As we climb higher this peace increases in a surprising manner. It becomes religious. In order not to disturb the concentrated state of the atmosphere, we no longer dare to think. The surroundings seem to become more subtle.

The speed of movement increases. The shadow of a thought evokes a whole world of phenomena. At last, if we go on with this strange ascent, a magnetic hyper-activity saturates the atmosphere. Soon we feel giddy. If we persist, it seems as if our basis of energy tends to disintegrate, owing to an inexplicable disturbance of the equilibrium. It would seem as if all the particles of our being were being violently torn apart, and this painful explosion forces the experimenter to descend into regions which are more favourable to his personal vibrations.

In the intermediate regions, the impression is better, the feelings more stable. One can compare the clearness of the atmosphere to the day at early morning. On the whole a sensation of repose, of confidence and calm is experienced. At the same time the consciousness receives various impressions. At certain stages there is neither joy nor sorrow. Other stages communicate to it a feeling of greater activity. One feels absolutely at home, one thinks or acts without any appreciable effort. The simple act of thinking will transport you wheresoever you wish. At times the atmosphere seems to be like velvet.

These observations were made during the first few years of study. When we have become able, by means of training and evolution of consciousness, to penetrate to the centrifugal states where the "pure energy" aspect of matter rules, the feelings become changed.

The task is always more arduous in those planes of matter which are darker and denser, but the consciousness no longer experiences any apprehension. It has acquired a certain stability which allows it to travel to the higher or lower states, without losing in the least its calmness and confident serenity. It acts without anxiety and without care, with a confident peace and a special sort of happiness which accompanies it. When the consciousness is directed towards the higher worlds, the impression felt may be described as the form of quiet happiness experienced by the traveller on returning home after a long absence. In this world, where cause and effect are one, the impression received is that of returning to a familiar place. Without thinking, one goes straight to the goal. One sees nothing, one does not think, and yet one feels by a kind of intuition, that the universe and its laws are at our disposal. And we use the faculties inherent in this state with the pleasure and ease of the traveller rediscovering familiar objects or favourite hobbies.

These general observations teach us that the punishments invented by man do not exist. Everyone finds, after death, the plane in which he can continue to exercise his affections. This does not mean to say that everybody will be happy, as one generally understands the term.

Here arises an important distinction. In the states where I made my observations, happiness or unhappiness are independent of the working of the universe. The law of Cause and Effect does not trouble itself with our preferences or sentiments. The law does not favour the ascetic—equilibrium is absolutely established. The same causes always produce the same effects, if they are put into action under the same circumstances. This happens on all the planes of the universe. It is left to us to conform to the law.

Freedom exists in the choice of a decision. Determinism comes into play in the execution of this decision, because a relation of Cause and Effect unites them, and because this relationship is the essential factor of the universal order.

In principle, everyone should find happiness, since their affections draw them to a plane where the vibrations correspond to their own rhythm. For the animal, or the savage as yet unconscious of his responsibilities, this is true. For a civilized person it is not true. There are, in fact, few people who have not some instinctive knowledge of a superior order of things. Whatever these experiences may be, each one finds more or less the particular or general qualities tending towards progress and perfection.

He, or she, who has allowed himself to become absorbed during life by satisfactions and enjoyments of a low order, will find himself after death in a plane where he will try to satisfy the same needs.

On the other hand, the presence of more spiritual characteristics will have given him certain vibrations favourable to the positive planes of pure energy.

A moment arrives when he becomes disturbed. He catches a glimpse of the grossness of his surroundings. I do not refer to the impure beings who come to bother him, but to the inferior quality of the plane. His punishment begins. In order to acquire the freedom, that he glimpses by this inspiration, he tries to escape from his own atmosphere. But, as he must first work out the sum of the energy which he has accumulated during his earthly life, it is often only after centuries of painful loneliness that he can at last escape from the chains which he himself has forged.

Each time you think of human evolution, never forget this double characteristic of the universe.

The electro-mechanical constitution of Universal Energy balanced in each of its waves of high and low pressure by an equal amount of matter, varies in the amount of energy and matter forming complementary parts.

It has also a rhythmical aspect, under the mastery of the law of Cause and Effect, which brings together vibrations of a similar nature.

As we are composed of a system of whirling atoms, functioning at one moment in an open circuit and at another in a closed circuit, it is up to us to direct our relationships in an intelligent manner in order that we may escape from the lower regions of the cosmic whirlpool.

Broadly, when an honest man dies, he finds himself in a medium corresponding to his affections, and it is in an atmosphere of peace and quietude that he exercises his joy of living. This happiness lasts until the energy which has been registered is exhausted. It will be necessary for him to return to earth, renew his store of energy, until he is centred on but one attraction, knows only one form of harmony; that is, one which is independent of all forms of energy.

When we have attained the highest vibrationary speed of our universe; that is to say, when human consciousness has sufficiently realized the great Causes of evolution and has localized all its affections in this, its presence on earth becomes unnecessary.

This state manifests a supreme dimension, penetrating all the others. The consciousness vibrates on the fundamental harmony of all forms of energy, of which it becomes, in a way, a conduit. It is at this moment that human freedom coincides with the characteristics which have been attributed to the gods of religion.

The following is one of the most curious states which I have ever experienced. After having reached a highly sublimated state of the ether, I was stimulating the life of the space around me by projecting my life energy into a considerable area. I experienced a sensation as if I were extending in all directions, as if I had been placed in the centre of a sphere. At the same time, I was as entirely in the total volume of expansion as I was entirely in each separate point of this strange organism.

Whilst being clearly conscious of my unity I had the impression of multiplying myself. This multiplication neither increased nor decreased my energy in the least.

Without moving, I could feel myself bridging incalculable distances by means of the velvety vibration which formed the limits of the immense sphere which was my new domain. This activity seemed to "awaken" in each atom of this super-ether an attraction which would collect around me and whose effect was to increase the sweetness and delicacy of my energy.

Without having to think, I was endowed with a kind of divine consciousness. The finest vibration, entering into the atmosphere thus vitalized, would immediately inform me of the details of its origin, while at the same instant I would act in the necessary way. There was no difference of time between the action and my resultant reaction. Action and reaction were simultaneous, in an immediate clairvoyance of all the details of Cause and Effect.

In order to act, I communicated an impulse from my whole being either to the mass or to the fraction. Whether this impulse took effect simultaneously or separately in the atoms of this magnetic field, it always acted in a proportion corresponding to the perturbing cause. And, strange as it may seem, all I experienced from this effect was a great happiness, without my energy either increasing or decreasing by one iota. Lastly, I would repeat that, whilst being fully conscious of my unity, I could not say that I was more in the centre than on the surface, or in any other part of this radiant sphere. In truth, I felt myself as all over the sphere with an equal intensity.

Imagination would never have dared to conceive a function, at once so complex and so simple, of the higher consciousness. All the expressions which I use in order to describe these results, limit and destroy their experimental value. This substance which becomes ourselves, the prerogatives which are attached to it, the profound Love which we feel, the inexpressible well-being which is concurrent with this love, all melt into one unity-multiplicity, of which one is perfectly conscious. At this point in its evolution human consciousness is a synthesis, having at its beck and call the different rhythms of the universal order whose harmonies it has known in its past experiences.

On reflection, it is, after all, natural enough. If we take away from our earthly life all the forms on which we lean, if we look at what is really left after the disappearance of the physical envelope, what can there be, in fact, apart from affinities for a certain type of atoms, whose different relationships form the diversities of bodies, under the guise of which manifests one equivalent energy, one identical universal method?

CHAPTER IV

ANALYSIS OF THE PHENOMENON OF SEPARATION
BETWEEN THE HUMAN BEING AND HIS BODY

In order to observe successfully the composition of Universal Ether, in its varying proportions of Energy and Matter, it is essential to start by keeping the memory clear from the beginning to the end of the experience.

The more we rise towards the rarefied higher ether the less we can depend on our memory. If the concentration of the will is not kept up sufficiently another source of error intervenes. The consciousness abandons its astral body. This latter, endowed with a certain sensitivity of consciousness, gauges impressions on its own plane, whilst the conscious spirit brings back impressions from another dimension. The result is a mixture, more or less coherent, of illusion and reality.

Therefore, the first point to be observed in the study of the fourth dimension is always to retain a conscious and continuous memory of the phenomena. In practice this control is very easy. You must act in the other dimensions of space with more certitude than on earth. That is to say, you must not only retain full mastery of your ordinary faculties, but your greater sensitivity permits a more

43

rigorous control. In good experimental conditions, faculties and sensations should be but one conscious unity, capable of judging, thinking, foreseeing, discerning, and acting with entire freedom.

For most people, the most convincing phenomenon is the act of conscious separation a few feet from the physical body. You leave your body with greater ease than taking off a suit of clothes and you wonder why this faculty is not more widespread. What a mass of stupid mistakes we could then avoid.

At all events, the result is a certainty, without the least doubt. It is a cold fact, beyond all judgment, beyond all hypothesis, hallucination, or suggestion. It is the most evident certitude obtainable, without any possibility of error.

As soon as we slip out of the physical wrapper this truth strikes us with all its force. We see the familiar furniture of our room just as before. The only difference we notice is a slight phosphorescent glow. Our physical body rests inert, like a corpse, on the couch. The impression is so striking that instinctively we think we are dead. We must avoid giving way to this natural reaction, and with all our will must resist the pull which wants to draw us back to our physical self. This double is so sensitive that an exaggerated fear would draw it back into its envelope with brutal suddenness, and we might find difficulty in trying the experiment again.

If we resist we have time to take note of surroundings, then we slowly re-enter our physical body and straightway note what we have observed. When this has been done we should try the same thing again. It will be much easier. The more the double becomes used to temporary disembodiment the easier it becomes to handle. We can then walk about in our room without inconvenience, making every possible and conceivable observation; we can sit down, think, and meditate with far greater lucidity than in physical consciousness.

At first we are tempted to leave our room in order to take stock of other places in this strange dimension. This is what happens: the substance which we are using to give form to our double returns to the physical body and it is with a far more ethereal body that we soar into space. The delicate nature of the vibrations in this new dimension gives access to quite a new order of phenomena. These should be observed with the most minute attention in order to become aware of the possibilities of each world into which we penetrate. If we wish to push the experiment still further it is possible to exteriorize a third body into an ether of even finer nature, and the phenomena develop in a proportionate manner.

Everything happens as if we had a series of different bodies boxed one in the other by means of a more reduced dimension. As the conscious will penetrates into new dimensions it uses a corresponding body.

As each of the successive states of this universe penetrates the inferior dimensions of the substance we have just quitted, it is easy to imagine the tremendous extent of phenomena which come within our orbit. To sum up, we draw near the fundamental causes of phenomena, and the same separation accomplished upon a higher plane causes a series of vibratory disturbances on lower levels, which in turn become causes in a substance still more condensed.

When we project ourselves in a way which lacks order and method, we are not properly aware of the nature of the body which exteriorizes itself. This means that the consciousness will not find itself in a proper medium for pure observation, and the results obtained will not agree with those of a student who has used the necessary vehicle for each stratum of consciousness.

From this we come to a second point which has to be noticed. Always start with the first projected double and then practice projecting yourself from that, inside your room, without trying to travel away.

The experiments which can be carried out in this dimension are many and varied. These allow us to obtain all kinds of new data about our present-day knowledge and to start building up facts concerning problems which are considered beyond solution by our modern civilization.

Also, the act of conscious separation itself, its absolute possibility, beyond all possible argument, whilst keeping control of all our perceptive faculties and feelings, is in itself quite enough to balance all our opinions concerning science, morality, and religion.

The phenomenon of dissociation between man and his body, the absolute certainty of being able to live in a new dimension, is the only obvious truth that I can claim as being true without the least doubt.

This certainty is in no way a dogma. It is not a matter of faith. It is not a case of auto-suggestion. It is a truth within the reach of all. It is the mathematically precise result, born from a series of causes, all ending in the same result, so long as they are practised in the same conditions. It is a fact beyond all reasoning, beyond all criticism and argument. To deny the possibility of such a feat, before having tried to do it oneself, would, in my eyes, simply be a proof of such an individual's lack of evolution, irrespective of his social status.

Apart from this certainty, I am offering you all further details as personal observations. There are, in fact, many very interesting points over which I have not lingered. I always wanted to know the last word of the puzzle—to attain the highest possibilities of consciousness, and the facts which have resulted therefrom are so marvellous that they will seem to be imaginary to those who are not aware of the admirable organization of the higher planes.

.   .   .   .

Let us, first of all, examine the nature of the sensations and impressions received during the process of dissociation. Despite their infinite variety they may be classified in three categories:

(1) Phenomena of sensation which prepare for the act of projection.

(2) Instantaneous projections which may or may not be accompanied by sensations.

(3) Projection by whirlwind.

The best time for observing these phenomena is about four to five in the morning, after having slept well. In this way we avoid the influence of the subconscious mind.

After having concentrated on all the details upon

which we wish to experiment, we drive away all thought and find ourselves in an excellent condition for receiving the weakest vibrations which come from the other dimensions of space.

Care must be taken not to fall asleep nor to be in this state even for a few seconds before contacting reality. As soon as a vibration, however weak it may be, affects one of our bodies, we must at once take full possession of ourselves. Our full attention must be immovably fixed on the sensations, images and scenes which are about to occur. We must be absolutely lucid, holding well in mind all the decisions previously made, and carefully following the different phases of the phenomenon, so that later on we may be able to note every detail. It is better to begin all over again fifty times in order to be able to record our observations, than to seek to put everything down at once. Remember that too much detail spoils the precision of facts.

After all, nothing could be easier, since we are not asleep. Projection, the separation of the conscious "I" and its provisional forms, takes place in full waking consciousness.

It has happened at times that I have found myself projected, standing beside my body, at the same instant as I closed my eyes, and without experiencing any particular sensation. Such speed is extraordinary. But what is most surprising is the reality of the material feelings one experiences. The practice of projection becomes such a habit that there have been times when I have come back to my body in order to make sure that I was really projected and not sleep-walking.

This will give you some idea of the striking reality

of this state.   Tell yourself that you are the conscious master of your different bodies.

The following experience will demonstrate the flexibility of this system, in transferring feeling from one form to another.

After having roamed about in space I came back close to my physical body and, without completely reincorporating myself, I found myself at the exact point of balance where the material sensitivity passes into the next body, or plane.   By a mere act of will I found myself able to incline the balance towards one point or the other.   As soon as I favoured the idea of projection into a fourth dimension I began to feel lighter, without any physical movement at all.   And, strangely enough, I had but one sensation, that is, as if my hands were touching behind my back in a familiar position.   As soon as I brought my mind back to my physical body the intensity of the projection diminished.   My body was as heavy as lead and breathing slowed down. I could feel the slight roughness of the sheets on my down-stretched arms next to my body, the freshness of the outside air, and the daylight which was filtering through my eyelids.   I could hear noises from the street.

Taking my mind back towards the idea of projection, the equilibrium immediately went the other way.   All these physical sensations disappeared with lightning-like speed.   I once more found myself in the state which I had just left, and began to enjoy the peace, the cool sweetness, and the inexpressible sense of well-being of this state.

The phenomenon of projection is not, therefore, a state of sleep, natural or induced.   It has a clarity far superior to that of terrestrial life. Whatever the dimension in which we find ourselves we must remain conscious, and be capable of opening our eyes at will, taking up a pencil and noting down whatever we may have observed, just as in our most alert waking moments.

CHAPTER V

THE general characteristic of the phenomena belonging to this category, is the preparation for the work which is going to take place, by activating one of the sensory faculties. Whether it be through images or feelings, it permits the student not yet fully familiar with that intermediate state which we might call self-isolation, to take full cognisance of himself and help the extraction of his double by acting in the right way.

We may use the image of a window, a door, anything which gives us the idea of passage from one place to another. It can also be a luminous area, a geometrical figure, a clear space in the midst of clouds, all evoking the same wish. One day I became conscious of my condition at a moment when I was half-projected. My face turned towards the floor, my body leaning slightly forward, my arms stretched out in front of me, I allowed myself to slip to the ground and "pulled" on that part of my double still fixed in its envelope, just as if I were sliding out of a coat that was too tight. Soon I experienced the feeling of placing my feet on the ground and stood up, regaining a normal posture, with that feeling of freedom which is so characteristic of the projected state.

Another time I had scarcely closed my eyes when I found myself half out of my body. My chest was stretched out, horizontally, off the bed, my face turned upwards towards the ceiling. The suddenness, and the lugubrious effect of this scene produced such a shudder that I immediately re-entered my physical form.

We must be ready for the strangest surprises. During one experiment, when I had used more effort than usual to project myself, I was hardly out of my body when I received a terrific slap in the face without being able to find whence it came.

Another time I was scarcely out of my body when I began to turn on my own axis, like "*looping the loop*," which was not at all pleasant. A further example, even more unpleasant, was a complete knocking over of the projected double. That day I had met unusual resistance in my projection exercises. The more I increased my efforts, the more I felt oppressed by the surrounding matter. Determined to conquer in spite of all obstacles, I concentrated all my will and was freed. Immediately I became aware of an intense disorganization in my astral body. I had a feeling of having every atom broken to pieces. As is my practice in case of difficulty, I called for help, when at once everything stopped and I returned to my body.

In this category the final sensation in which all others culminate, is that of "coming out" of something, of leaving a narrow, tight place. All our efforts should be directed to obtaining this result in varying degrees. Immediately on becoming free a feeling of well-being flows through us; we seem to breathe with greater ease; the consciousness has a feeling of unaccustomed freedom, and at the beginning I would find myself shaking myself like a dog just out of the water.

This is not always accomplished straightway. Sometimes one stays for an hour or two in a highly strung, nervous condition. The state of balance of the physical body, the general harmony of the psychological being, atmospheric conditions, heat, damp, or dryness, are all factors which play their part. All vibrations, whatever their nature, sound, light, electricity, other people near one, exert an influence on the production of the phenomenon. We must therefore be prepared for the most contradictory sensations, until we have discovered the most favourable conditions in our own case for the manifestation of projection.

One day I saw myself stretched out face down on a table, gripping and pulling at the edge, in order to leave my body. Another time, I found myself in bed, my head where my feet should have been; and I was moving in a jerky manner which was, then, necessary in order to obtain the desired results. On still another occasion I had the sensation of wrapping myself round the bedpost in order to leave my recalcitrant body.

In the foregoing examples vision and feeling are united. They can also be alternating, as in the cases already cited, or quite separate.

In certain cases I had the impression of dragging myself along the bed. Without seeing it I would feel my covering as a hindering roughness. During other experiments, I seemed to be touching the ceiling, and felt as if I were breathing through a thread. Then this breathing would become weaker and weaker until I gave one last leap forward and found myself in the next dimension.

A rarer type of experience is concerned with the psychic influence of our unseen guides. A sort of fine rain, exceedingly cold, pours on the body from head to foot, and slowly numbs it. Or else it seems as if circular mesmeric passes are being made over the face.

The result is always the same: a sensation of passing through a narrow opening, followed by a conscious projection in the vicinity of the physical body.

It may also happen that rather disagreeable visions of an hallucinatory character may be experienced. One day, with my eyes wide open, I saw a huge spider take shape beside me. On another occasion two small dogs appeared in the same way. Though less unpleasant than the former experience, I dismissed the apparition, as it was useless for the results I was seeking.

Generally the reactions of the sensory being are to be noticed just after projection, and whilst still near the body. When going forth into further dimensions the experiences are rather like those to be described in the following chapters. In every case, calm self-control is an absolute necessity. One must have sufficient self-mastery to be able to step aside and watch the phenomena as if they were happening to someone else.

CHAPTER VI

INSTANTANEOUS PROJECTION

THE phenomena of this second category pre-suppose a certain amount of practice. Nevertheless, as they may happen when they are least expected, it is wise to know about them in order not to be taken by surprise.

Their main characteristic lies in the lightning-like speed with which projection takes place. When feeling accompanies this type of projection it seems as if we were being hurled through space. There are times, though, when there is no feeling, and we just find ourself projected, either in the room or in another dimension.

It is here more than ever necessary for the consciousness to be prepared for this speedy transit, so that it may be ready to take up the defensive. We never know the nature of the phenomenon which may occur, and it is always wise to exercise prudence.

During one of these experiences I had the un-pleasant sensation of being hurled head first into space. There is naturally at first a moment of surprise which we must do our best to reduce as far as possible. The consciousness must immediately acquire its full lucidity and be ready to counter whatever obstacles may be put in its way.

Another day, contrary to my usual custom, I had projected myself lying on my right side. I felt as if I were falling suddenly, as if I had been lying on a trap-door which had been suddenly opened under me. My first impulse was automatically to make the same movements as would occur if this had happened to my physical body. I stretched out my arms and legs in the hope of gripping something, and started to cry out. However speedy this reaction may be it has the effort of producing clarity of consciousness. I recovered my presence of mind, became fully conscious of my projected condition, of the efforts which I had already made, of the essentials for success, and the possible hindrances, and of the decisions I had made, all of which I noticed without resisting the process of projection.

In another set of experiments I had been neatly blocked by contrary forces. I struggled as hard as I could, but only succeeded in coming away with a general bruised feeling. On the day following this struggle I had not yet finished concentrating, when my astral body was shot out violently like a shell from a gun. I was thrown out, face downwards, with my arms stretched out, so realistically that I thought that I had really been thrown from my bed to the floor. There was nothing to give cause for worry. I was well out of my body and proceeded to carry out, in my room, the experiments I had in mind. As it happened, on that day my astral double was more condensed than usual. In order to change to another dimension I tried to pass through the walls of the room, but found that they resisted my efforts. When I tried harder I only managed to produce a pain in my forehead and had to resort to the astral opening of the window before my first projection could have its way.

Another time, after having seen several grinning shapes, I found myself standing up in my room quite without preparation. The surprise was all the greater as I had not thought to project myself, and had prepared no programme.

In another case, I experienced a sensation of nameless fear. All my conscious faculties became limp, and suddenly I realized that I was in an unpleasant greyish atmosphere like dense clouds. Rising perpendicularly in this sombre mass, which made no appeal to me, I kept on the defensive (as in these states one may be attacked by rather unpleasant entities), whilst travelling with all possible speed. I then came to a more sympathetic stratum where I found one of my deceased friends with whom I had a fairly long conversation.

What is particularly pleasant in these visits is the absence of the hypocrisy with which our earthly relationships are poisoned. Nothing can express the delicacy of the sentiments shared and understood in our relations with our Friends of Space.

In order to appreciate this properly you must remember that I am not telling you a dream, nor a vision. I am telling you of a real fact, a conscious act accomplished with an absolutely clear mind, with perfect freedom, and without any trace of sleep. You are there near your friends, talking affectionately, fully conscious of your double state, which you can terminate immediately whenever you wish. As all your psychical elements are active, a thought is all that is needed to bring you straight back to your body with a lucidity equal to that of any moment of the day.

On the contrary there are times when you will feel rejuvenated by this more intense life.

As a matter of fact one often retains traces of the radio-active principles of the worlds one explores. These extra vibrations give one splendid strength and energy. We think and act during the day with unparalleled ease. Without effort, complicated problems are solved. But, the strangest thing about this state is the way we take it for granted. Do not think that we are wonderstruck. This state seems so natural that it is as if it had always been the case, and there seems to be no end to it. I have noticed that this feeling of perfect calm is realized with an intensity proportionate to the height, and refinement of the strata of ether to which we have penetrated. Maximum power is attained during the union of the Higher Consciousness and the Essence of the Life Spiritual.

It is only after having returned to the normal state that the difference can be appreciated. It seems as if all our faculties are shut up in a box, while thought only filters painfully through the molecules.

Among the cases of instantaneous projection I once had the ordinary feeling of getting up in the morning. As there is no difference in ordinary waking, one does not notice what has happened. It is only when one is standing up, conscious that the physical body is still on the bed, that the double state is realized.

Lastly, the most curious of the experiences in this category is the following. I awakened as usual and, having noted the time, lay down as usual with my arms by my side. I was getting ready to shut my eyes and prepare myself by different psychical exercises when immediately I found myself standing beside my body without having had time even to close my eyes. For a moment I was startled, looking at my outstretched body with its open and expressionless eyes. During this attempt there was not the slightest alteration in the memory or the conscious faculties. Without any time-interval the sensory power of my physical body passed into the double, and all the faculties followed straightway.

CHAPTER VII

PROJECTION BY WHIRLWIND

THE separation between the conscious being and his organic envelope takes place under a strange impulse in this third category, giving the impression of being lifted up by a whirlwind. The sensation of being sucked up violently by a sort of huge vortex is felt, and there is an immediate and conscious contact with the other worlds. This extraction from the body is never painful. But, as we are generally unaware of the spot on which the whirlwind is going to drop us, it is wiser to stay on the defensive.

In order to keep better control, I made it a habit to project myself into my room before soaring to other dimensions. However, this whirlwind is not always obedient and often it sucks up a more ethereal body, which it carries away in an etheric "draught" which is extraordinarily interesting to experience. This is undoubtedly the most agreeable of all forms of projection. Though it can be attached to all sorts of visions and sensations this is not essential. Generally the sensory reactions which follow this type of projection are more delicate and refined. The expenditure of energy is not noticeable. The faculties are more alert.

Thought is far quicker. A far more homogeneous unity of life is experienced, whose more vibrant activity transmits to the consciousness influences which are unknown in other dimensions.

Here are a few examples. Having awakened at the usual time for my experiments, I was surprised to hear tremendous barkings all around me. Immediately I felt myself being carried away in a whirlwind. I had the feeling of descending rapidly. In the greyish and cloudy opacity of the atmosphere into which I plunged I noticed greenish glows and, next to me, a big white dog. Then the current slowed down bit by bit and led me back into my body. I immediately noted down what had happened and awaited a new experience. I did not have to wait long. A sort of fine ice-cold rain was falling on my head with great intensity and soon I was drawn from my body by a whirlwind whose duration was as short as the first. After having, once more, made a note of its main characteristics, I waited for a third experience. This time the fluids were less intense. I was travelling through space upright, floating a few feet from the earth. This happened during 1914, and I visited Belgium and viewed the horrors of war in this manner.

In passing, note the white dog as a symbol of the means used by the Friends who help us during our psychic experiments. Actually, unless one has a special connection with them, the guides rarely show themselves. They would rather send an image which inspires confidence, and that of a dog is the most frequent. These dogs are not always white. They are sometimes grey, like sheep-dogs, and their size may vary from that of the little

Japanese dogs to that of great Saint-Bernards. There may be several dogs watching over us in this way, and their presence inspires both confidence and increases energy.

During the majority of cases projection by the whirlwind method is not accompanied by any visions or sensations. We are merely transported on a wind of ether, at a variable speed, towards some unknown goal. We must keep ourselves in readiness for any eventuality. When we are carried away by this magnetic current there is a feeling of tremendous speed. A howling tempest deafens our ears, as if we were travelling over the earth at a rate impossible to gauge. Several times I have noticed a white luminous cloud trailing my double.

The speed at which we are carried away may not allow us to put ourselves in a convenient position. Our double may be standing up, lying on the stomach, on the back, on the side, or simply sitting, as if in a chair. It may happen that we are transported head first, or feet first, in an horizontal, oblique, or vertical current, with the feeling of either rising or going down. Generally, when the current is lateral we may have confidence, but when the current is vertical, with a sensation of falling, it is time to be careful.

For example: in one experiment I was watching a lovely panorama unfold beneath me, when suddenly, without apparent motive, the current on which I was being carried suddenly changed its direction and I had the feeling of falling at a dizzy speed. I noticed many different images. The last was a sort of tube in which I was shut up. The further I went the narrower became the tube, with sensations corresponding. I had the feeling of being crushed in and was literally suffocating. Keeping cool, I began to smile, and mentally called my guides. Soon a whirlwind rushed me clean out of this disagreeable situation and, with a sigh of relief, I found myself in free space.

Travel in these electro-magnetic currents gives the feeling of being borne by a tremendous draught, at a dizzy speed, through a cloudy medium which is generally of a greyish nature, and through rifts in which various landscapes are seen. To be carried through a clear atmosphere is a much rarer occurrence.

These etheric currents to some extent revitalize the physical body. After other kinds of projection we sometimes suffer from lassitude or discomfort. This is rare in the present category. On the contrary, we return to the physical body feeling overcharged with vital energy. However banal the facts noticed may have been, the return is always accompanied with a more active, livelier consciousness. The most minute details are extraordinarily clear. The whole of the body is impregnated with an energy which is, at once, so gentle and yet so powerful that tears spring to the eyes. It is impossible to express adequately a state of happiness so complete, so real, and so vivid. Any form of earthly exaltation is a poor analogy, because we have never been so peaceful and calm before. It is, in some way, a higher life which pours into the physical form and gives, momentarily, a considerable increase to the range of our faculties.

The exceptional lucidity brought about by this kind of projection has its balancing factor, in that memory of it disappears all too quickly. It is an excellent habit immediately to make a note of what has happened if one wishes to keep a record. One day when I had delayed putting down my experiences I was only able to recover the memory of them by working backwards from the last to the first stages. Another time, with every detail of my experience absolutely clear in my mind, I had hardly put pencil to paper when memory vanished in a flash, and I was unable to remember the least detail. The following are further examples of projection by whirlwind.

After having stayed awake for an hour in the state of nervous tension which often precedes projection I felt myself being suddenly sucked up by a whirlwind. Not knowing where I was, seeing nothing, I called out for help and, without delay, found myself in my own room. A strange, rosy light illuminated the atmosphere. As soon as I had obtained full self-consciousness and noted what I would do, an etheric wind picked me up and carried me away among grey clouds. Lying on my back, without having to make any movement, I had a wonderful feeling of calm and security. The consciousness, endowed with a greater clarity than in my usual experiments, made it possible for me to notice everything more easily. No sensation, however weak, could pass me by. Whilst being quite free, without any faculty dominating another, my consciousness was impregnated by a sort of clairvoyant intuition, and I had the feeling that all the knowledge I had ever had was there, ready to manifest itself. I had the feeling that every atom was awake, experiencing a conscious unity of their powers, while no foreign vibration came to trouble the harmony of such a certitude.

I was carried for many miles over country familiar to my childhood. I went through material objects as if they had been imaginary pictures and then, having gone over many details of my youth, the current seemed to slow down and brought me back to my body.

In itself there is nothing very extraordinary in this projection. What gives it value in my eyes is the super-clarity, the super-lightness, and super-consciousness that I experienced.

On another occasion I was caught up by one of those magnetic currents during my projection. Contrary to my habit, I was experimenting during the evening and, after seeing a few grimacing faces, I found myself lightly deposited in my own room. After having walked up and down a little I noticed nothing worthy of interest. My astral body seemed to be lightly coloured, and as for my physical body, lying inert, it interested me not at all. I decided to go to a spot on the earth, hundreds of miles away, and passed through the wall of my room. I had hardly done this when I was swept up by a violent whirlwind and carried at a tremendous speed in a black cloud. I found myself travelling lying down and, as this blackness did not appeal to me, I tried to stand up, but could not. My astral body began to turn as if doing straight somersaults, and I continued to travel through space in this strange manner.

I called for help, and this painful situation coming to an end, I once more regained a normal position. The cloud disappeared and I passed, at the same fantastic speed, through a whole series of houses. During this experience I noticed a phosphorescent streak left in the wake of my body. At last the current slowed down and I regained my physical body.

CHAPTER VIII

CONSCIOUSNESS SEPARATED FROM THE PHYSICAL BODY

To separate oneself into two distinct parts, in familiar surroundings, acting in full waking consciousness, with more than the freedom and thinking power of an entity living on earth, sums up the greatest triumph the thinking "I" can gain over matter.

There are no limits to this triumph. Human consciousness can, if it so wishes, penetrate a series of dimensions in what we know as space, reaching up to the highest plane, which coincides with the fundamental state manifested by the atoms of our particular universe.

Our ordinary knowledge, our education, our moral system, and our social customs being in flagrant contradiction with this experimental reality, we experience at our first attempts at projection a shock for which we must be ready.

Truth is so sudden and brutal that our human vocabulary fails before the accomplished fact. Before such evidence, which we doubt right up to the last moment, all the self-contradictory reasonings of science, religion and philosophy, collapse pitifully, leaving not a trace behind. At the same time a flood of "whys" and "hows" rises up from every quarter, and this superabundance of ideas gives a feeling of being struck on the head with a club. This state only lasts a short while. Soon the success of so problematic an experiment, the intimate, overwhelming joy of knowing at last the reality, apart from any sentimental and intellectual speculation, gives the student that hope and certainty of which civilization had robbed him.

What is most astonishing about this experience is the speed with which all ordinary knowledge disappears. Immediately reduced to nothing, this bursts like a bubble. At once we stand aghast at the efforts which, for centuries and centuries, have been made by man in order to bring about this final catastrophe. However, if we reflect, we realize that it is this very human uncertainty which has led us to make the efforts necessary to reach the experimental certainty of to-day.

Once the first surprise has passed we begin to leave with joy the prison of flesh. In this new domain we look around at our familiar surroundings with pleasure. We walk about our room with an unaccustomed feeling of strength and confidence. Our ideas are more precise than in earthly life. In short, it is a life inconceivably better than terrestrial existence.

At each experiment the same joys come again. The main impression we receive is one of returning to a well-loved home after a long absence. And this impression, this confidence, this feeling of home-coming is proportionate to the quality of "energy" of the matter into which we project ourselves.

The body which projects itself in this way and stands next to the physical body is, to some extent, material. It is made up of sensory matter from our physical being and cannot go further than a few yards away. It is therefore natural that in this state we would continue the acts and gestures of our physical form. Thus, in order to leave the room we must simulate the acts of opening doors or windows. Time and again I have tried to pass through walls in this state and have only managed to give myself a headache, just as if I had banged my physical head against a wall. Much later on I was successful. At first the walls felt soft, and then I went through them as if they were not there at all. But that was only because I exteriorized a less material double, far more radio-active than the previous ones.

The atmosphere of the room follows the same variations. A weak phosphorescence gives a special luminosity. Though rather dark it is quite easy to find one's way about. When the magnetic sensitivity of the double increases, so also does the light. The following are a few examples of projection which I accomplished in my room.

One evening I tried an experiment without bothering to undress, merely lying down on my bed. I simply began to think about projecting myself, without undertaking any other exercises, and closed my eyes. Soon an image came clearly before my sight. I made the necessary effort and experienced a feeling as if I were wriggling through a tight opening. At last, in my second body, I rose from my bed. Despite the fact that I had been practising projection for over a year, as soon as I left my body I felt an instinctive fear. I mastered myself, but despite my will, the suggestion of fear had done its work. It seemed as if thousands of invisible threads were trying to pull me back into my physical body. I resisted with all my might and looked curiously around me. All was dark. The fire in the grate was giving a dim light, and I noted that, contrary to the statements of several writers on this subject, the walls were not transparent. With my right hand I gripped my left wrist; it seemed quite solid. At that moment I heard a familiar tune being whistled. Though I could not see anything I felt that this was meant for my ears. However, the pull had not ceased and I was forced to give way. I opened my eyes, took notes of what had happened, undressed, went to bed, and started a new experiment.

I had concentrated my mind on the following: To bring a piece of paper from the chest of drawers to my bed, and to examine my surroundings more attentively. I fell asleep and awoke towards midnight with a vague memory of having flown, at a great height, over some buildings. Looking at the time, I once more closed my eyes. I had hardly done this than I left my body in a rather strange manner. I was standing balanced on my hands and, in this manner, walked around the room with my feet in the air. Reaching my bed again, I took up the normal posture. Now, although the fire had gone out, the room seemed less dark than the first time. I felt very peaceful. Nothing distracted my attention. Remembering what I had decided to do I went towards the chest of drawers but saw two pieces of paper instead of one. I picked up both of them and put them on the bed. Then, still in my astral body, I sat down in my armchair to meditate on this strange happening. I examined my hands and feet. They seemed semi-material, as if seen under X-rays. Finally, not seeing anything else of interest, I decided to transfer the consciousness to another dimension and visit a friend. I stepped on to the balcony, and with a light leap found myself in the street. I had not gone fifty yards before an irresistible pull drew me back, and I was forced to re-enter my body. I opened my eyes, wrote down the details of the experiment and, looking up, noted that the piece of paper had not moved from the chest of drawers where I had originally put it.

Towards three o'clock in the morning I attempted a third projection. This time the atmosphere was still more luminous. Although the shutters were closed I could see a fine blue sky through them. I once again began my experiment. I blew on that decidedly recalcitrant piece of paper. I examined my arms and, as on the previous occasion, found them to be solid to the touch and surrounded by a grey aura just as in an X-ray photograph. Then, to finish up, I re-entered my body. The piece of paper had not moved at all.

Ever since I began these experiments I have noted the possibility of projecting a double whose density would vary considerably, bringing in its wake all sorts of experimental powers and possibilities.

During another exercise of the same kind I became aware of myself by a definite slowing down of the breath, followed by the sensation of trying to squeeze through a narrow space. Then I felt more free and was no longer cramped. This time the room seemed rather dark. I contemplated without enthusiasm my physical body, whose shape showed through the bed-covers. I touched it;   eemed

soft. I kissed myself and came away with the
feeling of having kissed someone who had only been
dead a short time. In the midst of this rather transparent darkness this tepid body, limp and inert,
has a rather lugubrious appearance. However, I
brought back to mind my original intention in projecting myself, which was to travel to a spot some
twelve miles away, in order to visit a friend. With
this purpose I went towards the window. As I
tried to pass through it I was met by a resistance
which I could not conquer. I thought that my projected double must be too material, and therefore
made pretence of opening the window and flung
myself into space thinking of the person I wished to
visit. My journey was quite speedy. Repeatedly I
felt fatigued and was forced to stop, but after having
prayed, strength flowed back to me and I arrived at
the end of my journey without difficulty. I kissed
the person in question, who pointed out to me that I
possessed neither stomach nor feet. I answered,
telling her that in this dimension one only kept the
appearance of the upper portion of the body. I
noticed that talking was trying me a great deal. As
soon as I stopped speaking, strength seemed to come
back. At last I came back to my body, calmer and
stronger than when I began the experiment.

With regard to the question of "*time*" it should
be noted that its value is in an inverse ratio to the
radio-activity of the stratum in which one projects
oneself. Time becomes instantaneous in the pure
essence of the higher worlds. Prayer, too, is a word
from which we should strip all its superstitious
dressing. In the invisible worlds prayer is synonymous
with calling, with asking for help and protection.

The following is another projection accomplished with a body whose vibrations were still more subtle.

Without preliminaries I simply thought about projecting myself. I became aware of myself in the very act of projection. I had both the feeling and the vision of lying face down on a table. My arms were stretched out in front of me and I was pulling on the edges of this imaginary table to free myself from something. I had the impression of being in a sack whose narrow opening was no more than a crack. At last my efforts were crowned with success and I found myself standing next to my body in full possession of all my faculties. For a while I watched myself sleeping. Then I kissed my wife and children and went off towards the East. For some time I floated in a normal position; that is to say, standing up in an atmospheric medium, my body leaning forward slightly, my head well forward with my face turned towards the horizon, if I make myself clear. All of a sudden I felt a pull which put me on my back, and drew me, feet first, in an unknown direction. Without losing my self-control I let myself go, at the same time redoubling my attention. I came to a place in space which was represented by a room. Several people were sitting round a sleeping man. I was told the name of the sick man and invited to sit down, when I chatted with my neighbour on different things. I then left the company and re-entered my body in order to put down notes of what had happened. The topics of our conversation, however, disappeared from my memory.

I now freed myself again from my physical body.

I then saw my Guide to whom I put several questions, the answers to which, this time, I remembered. Finally, instead of going, as usual, straight back into my body, I stopped in my room in order to notice the difference between a fairly condensed projection and a far more rarefied substance such as the one I had just been using. The surrounding atmosphere of the room was far more luminous than usual. I saw my wife turn over in bed without having the slightest reflex. Then I practised going in and out of my physical envelope. The tenuity of the exteriorized form allowed me to do this without effort. This double followed the impulse of my thoughts with amazing facility. I hardly formed the idea that I wanted to return to my body when, immediately, I clearly felt the bed on which I was lying. The weight of my limbs, the difficult and feeble breathing, the cold air, the thousand-and-one street noises, all told me that I was back again in my physical form. Did I wish to leave it? Like a flash all those feelings disappeared. I could see my body stretched out on the bed, and could walk about the room with greater ease than usual. After I had repeated this exercise as many times as I wished, I opened my eyes, which act in no way hindered the detailed precision of my observations.

CHAPTER IX

THE CONNECTING CORD

WHATEVER may be the density of the atoms of the substance which we use to penetrate into other dimensions, the connection between the physical body and its more subtle double is maintained by means of a kind of cord. The extent to which this cord can stretch seems to be limitless, and it resembles the trail of a rocket as it soars into space. Where the cord joins the double it consists of thousands of very fine, elastic threads, which seem to suck the double into them.

To make a detailed study of this point, it is important to practise re-entering the body very slowly. The nearer we come to our physical body the more we feel those ties which draw us back, which pump us, so to speak; and it seems as if we were irresistibly melting into our body. The stronger this feeling becomes the more we feel the material sensation of the physical being. First of all these sensations seem far away, then they become stronger and stronger until we are reabsorbed completely into the physical body.

Subsequent upon several experiments, the following axiom seems to stand out: the *"Rapport"* existing between the physical body of a human being

75

and the matter of his other bodies is in an inverse ratio to the electro-magnetic power of the said matter.

In other words, the double is the more tied to the physical body the more crude, or material, its composition. The transmission of vibrations from the one to the other follows the same progression. This explains the wounds or deaths of those unhappy sorcerers and witches whose projected form was too dense in quality, and would therefore transfer any blows or wounds it might receive to the physical body.

As we penetrate into the upper regions the easier it becomes to separate the conscious form from the physical body; so that the projection of the spiritual essence of man is the act demanding the minimum of effort. On the other hand, this calls for a very special training in order to free the Higher Consciousness from its ties with lower forms of matter.

When I first began my experiments I noticed several times the difficulties caused by using a double of too material a quality. Everything bothers one. All the vibrations which affect the body touch the double with magnified intensity. The sensory reactions of the projected form are all of a material order. The fluidic cord which ties the two bodies together follows the same law and is also very highly sensitized. The intimacy of the relationship between a body of dense matter and its next refinement has allowed me to try out experimentally curious cases of ubiquity.

The following is an example: whilst projected I was passing over a magnificent countryside, the whole panorama seeming to be lit up by brilliant sunshine. I could distinguish every detail. I arrived by the sea, the waves of which were beating against the shore, and sat down on some cement steps near which some children were playing. With delight I breathed the salt air, whilst a fresh wind caressed my face. Now, the definitely material feelings of this state were complicated by other vibrations transmitted by the astral cord. During this projection someone was walking in the room and each step on the floor produced reverberations in my astral body which each time drew me nearer my physical form. I was fully conscious of these simultaneous states and, while tasting of the pleasure of this projection, my will strove vigorously against the pull of these thousands of invisible ties. Finally, I succumbed, and was forced to return to my room.

The bald recital of this state of dual consciousness cannot give the least idea of the truth. Remember that I was all the time fully aware of the fact that I could end or prolong my projection. At the same time I was fully alive to the attractions which were trying to draw me back and was looking about for a means of minimizing them. For the time being my will conquered, but, in the end, I was forced to give way.

Here again it is a matter of training, and it is possible to neutralize this annoying sensitivity on the part of the astral cord.

CHAPTER X

WHILST the experimenter is merely projecting himself into his own room, strolling about there, walking down to the front door and out into the street, there is no real difference between the acts performed in the astral and those performed in the physical state. But, when it becomes a matter of hurling oneself into space it is quite another matter.

First of all, before trying this, it is necessary to make sure that your physical body is still in the same place. Suppose for a moment that you are sleep-walking and that you live on the sixth floor. The arc which you would draw in space might be graceful, but the end would be somewhat lacking in charm.

As we have not developed the habit of gliding in the air like a bird, I first of all began by making the movements of swimming. It was therefore by pretending to swim that I first travelled in space.

Little by little my skill improved. Instead of swimming in the usual way, using the breast-stroke, I began to move along with a sort of side-stroke. After that I learnt to turn over on my back and float, pushing with my feet only. Finally, I would travel horizontally, with my hands clasped together and arms stretched out as if to cut through the ether which lay before me, impelled simply by a wish.

When travelling above a material surface, or an ethereal surface which takes on a material shape, the impression of being surrounded by a great void is far less strong. It will, in such cases, be found quite a simple matter to glide, standing up, without the help of any gesture.

The fear of empty space which is experienced at the beginning is due to the formidable sense of reality with which this conscious projection strikes one. During a dream one would feel no fear. Whilst dreaming such a feat would seem quite natural. But here, though, in full possession of the ordinary consciousness, which has been transferred from the physical envelope to the astral double, there is undoubtedly ground for hesitation.

In this new state, of which at first it is quite ignorant, the ordinary consciousness soon gains confidence through the use of its new powers. The more these are exercised, the more quickly confidence is gained. Generally speaking, however, it is only after several years of training in the different dimensions that our consciousness manages to discern the reality and value of the scenes it sees, the power of thought and of the things which this can accomplish.

The ease with which the double travels also follows a similar line of progression. According as the double that one manages to project becomes finer, so do all the normal faculties obtain a proportionate development. Not only does it become unnecessary to make any gesture indicative of whatever movement or act we wish to make, but the very thought of movement, in the physical sense, disappears.

On one occasion, charged with a commission in a certain region of space, I noted the following characteristics. I was going to accomplish the work which had been entrusted to me without thinking which way I should go. The atmosphere in which I found myself, of a kind of light grey, seemed to have no limits. I went hither and thither, climbed up and down, laterally and obliquely, in all directions, all without thinking about it. In fact I was travelling to the spot where my work called me in the most natural manner. These movements, I might add, took place as instinctively as when moving an arm or a leg in the material world. I felt myself definitely master of that space which seems so unconquerable when we are on earth. The position in which I normally hold myself is as follows: It seems as if I were standing up, leaning slightly forward. In this way I float in the ether, looking straight in front of me. Then when I change from one dimension to another, I maintain a certain slope, as though following a tangent in a sphere.

In projection by whirlwind, the force of the current which draws one along prevents any idea of making a movement. It is irresistible. The most that can be done, and that is not always possible, is to stand up, one arm straight in front, the index and middle fingers held up as if giving a benediction. That is called the defence position. No fear should be felt. Let yourself be carried along. I have already told you the positions which should be avoided. For instance, to be drawn along, feet up in the air, either in an upward or downward direction, is undesirable.

I also experimented with quite a novel method of travelling, and this in a state where all notion or feeling of "time" had completely disappeared. The process seemed to be akin to that used in long-distance shooting, where the shell is launched on a calculated trajectory in order to fall on a predetermined spot. I came to this idea in working on one of the conceptions of the theory of relativity, which presupposes a super-ether beyond the material one, which would transmit vibrations quite independent of those of the more material ether, in which case a series of waves having crossed the material ether at the speed of light would, in the super-ether, have a speed of "x."

Here is an account of what happened. I had arranged a whole series of experiments in my room for that day. I was to knock a ball from a piece of furniture, put my finger-prints on a plate powdered with flour, etc. However, as soon as I was projected I changed my mind in regard to my intentions. I decided instead to call on a person living hundreds of miles away. Quietly poised, and well balanced in mind, I made my way towards the wall of the room, with the intention of passing through it. Suddenly a window, consisting of one large pane of glass, and without any means of opening, placed itself before me by some mysterious means. Experience having taught me the nature of such a raised-up obstacle, placed there by some unknown power, I was in no way afraid. Stretching forward my right arm, and pointing, I slowly made the sign of the cross on this image. The window disappeared, but was soon replaced by another. I repeated the sign, with the same result, and with the appearance of a third window. For the third time I repeated the protective sign. My movement was hardly finished when the window vanished, and, immediately, without the slightest perceptible lapse of time, I found myself hundreds of miles away. Combined with a speed which was in strong contrast to that which I usually experienced, it was impossible to doubt the reality of what had happened. I was in a street of the town where lived the person I was seeking, and as I walked towards the house, I meditated on this instantaneous means of transport. At the same time I noticed in myself a feeling of lightness, of clarity, and of hyper-consciousness, such as I had never before experienced so intensely. As I was not sure of the exact spot where my friend was living, I was suddenly drawn towards the second floor of an unknown house. There I found the individual I sought. I took stock of the furniture and the way it was distributed, and noted, in passing, that workmen were repairing the street.

On my return to the physical body, I once more freed myself again with an unaccustomed ease. A light zephyr carried me through space in obedience to the slightest impulse from my will. When I had returned to normal consciousness I retained the impression of the radio-active waves of this superior state for a whole day. No words of mine would do justice to the condition of superior consciousness experienced in this dimension. One carries clearly in mind even the most minute particulars of the experience, with an unimaginable wealth of detail, all without having to make the least effort. No mist, however light, intrudes upon the freedom and clarity of this perfect super-dimensional state.

I wrote to the individual in question, giving details of what I had seen so many miles away and, two months later, received full confirmation.

On the whole, the result of my experiments in the higher matter is that the soul travels at a speed proportionate to the quality of the "pure Energy" in which it finds itself. At the positive extremity of this quality one reaches instantaneousness. Time and space which are so greatly differentiated in this world of ours unify more and more in the greater refinement of other dimensions. The centrifugal extension of the atoms increases the extent of the circumscribed space. Time loses its value and instantaneousness is the ultimate quality of unity. This unity follows a trajectory which is on a plane at a tangent to the extreme limit of our universe.

CHAPTER XI

HOW THE HUMAN CONSCIOUSNESS USES ITS POWERS

TAKING into consideration the characteristics of the different invisible states of matter, the narration of my experiments gives only an approximate conception of the real thing. The factors which are of real worth in these unknown regions of the ether are almost untranslatable.

The unity of all thoughts, of judgment and sensory reactions, the freedom and power which are characteristic of this state, call for the use of faculties which are unknown down here. There is no simple expression to define them. This synthesis of faculties brings along a whole series of delicate and varied sensations. If to this one adds states of consciousness of tremendous scope, there follows an incredible clarity of multiple effects, based upon the few causes which bring them about. The further one penetrates into the more subtle states of matter, the further does this lucidity increase, to attain its absolute fullness at that point where our own universe contacts the Infinite, to which it gravitates.

In this supreme state, man has become a god, fecundating his portion of the universe with the

84

conscious life, of which he has now become both the centre and the circumference.

In the Invisible, the human being is represented by a state of consciousness. All the forms of expression, all the qualities, all the different faculties, by means of which one is able to define a human being, collect, ultimately, in this great synthetic unity called consciousness.

This consciousness judges, meditates, and acts with a freedom and lucidity proportionate to the sum of attraction which it is capable of bringing to bear. As this totality of attractions increases, the causes which bring them about decrease, or vice versa. At the final summing up, the consciousness discovers itself at the top of the latter, living in a maximun state of pure "Energy," in a radio-active unity, with free access to the phenomenal multiplicity of causes and effects in all their dimensions.

The universal order which allows access to such superlative powers is the only God which the human being will meet during his peregrinations. It is by Him that one has access to the world of phenomena. It is He who allows these strange faculties to be shut away in the majority of people. Again it is He, this Universal Order, which, in the infinity of all-including space, as in the basic atom of all the worlds in the cosmos, allows the evolution of life and of consciousness.

In order to help you to obtain a clear idea of the results of experiment, let us suppose that an engineer has at his disposal a special keyboard which represents the directing influences of the world. Each touch would correspond to a whole class of phenomena. Suppose, also, that the touches on this keyboard are gradually reduced and that the mighty "ensemble" of cause and effect to which it corresponds is set into vibration under the influence of will. In order to make our analogy complete, we must imagine that the musician has quite a free mind, without any dominant thought. We must see him acting without effort, with absolute certainty, without a shadow of hesitation, mechanically controlling his impulses in the direction, at the place, and following the true nature of the equilibrium to be brought about.

What is remarkable and quite beyond the understanding of us earth-dwellers is that, in the Invisible, it is within reason to imagine such possibilities without their author being tormented by a surging flood of ideas. The more we draw near to the directing influences of the world, the more the conscious spirit of man frees itself from the bonds of the multitudinous attractions of which the universe is composed. We might say definitely that the human being condenses himself into an infinitesimal Point, which could be defined as a state of Consciousness at rest.

The most mighty imagination will fail to conceive the dynamic intensity of the energy so constituted. Only experience in these high regions of being will allow us to realize that if human consciousness is able to put the forces of the cosmos into motion, it is precisely because it has cast off all form, to re-absorb itself into one of the fundamental principles of the universal order, of which it (the consciousness) has now become a conscious channel.

On earth memory is indispensable if we wish to

go deeply into the causes which underlie phenomena. In the invisible world this memory is replaced by the super-sensitivity of the "matter" into which we penetrate. The body of whirling atoms used by the consciousness vibrates in harmony with this matter and transmits to its creator whatever wave-lengths may be brought to birth.

Imagine the development, the very perfection, of such a system. Then you will realize the perfect union which exists between consciousness and the medium in which it manifests. In its growing rare-faction, the ether increases in that vital sensitiveness which allows it to touch inferior strata. Without being absorbed by it, its own dimension penetrates all others, and we can consider human consciousness as capable of localizing itself in each atom of this super-sensitive state of the universe.

This hypothesis will give you the key to the powers which one can observe in the invisible world. The practical result corresponds, in fact, to a progressive and clairvoyant sensitivity, bringing about a far more extended range of action. This sensitivity gives birth to a scale of sensations, the incredible delicacy of which gives the consciousness all the knowledge it could possibly require. At the very instant that such knowledge comes to the consciousness the latter has already acted in the necessary sense, by the help of inexplicable faculties, which are summed up in a form of autogenous impulse.

There is no beginning or end between perception and action. To perceive is to act and vice versa. And, every time we use this strange power, we have the impression of giving ourselves absolutely and without reserve, however small or great the space in which our consciousness is functioning.

We might compare the accuracy and delicacy with which actions are accomplished in this state, to the work of a clockmaker. When he sets about putting a watch together he does not consider the movements he is about to make in order to assemble each piece in its right place. Through habit he will place his cogs in the right and proper order whilst concentrating his full attention on the idea of placing them accurately. If he knows his job, it will be impossible for him to make a mistake. Each part is allocated to a predetermined position. They are not interchangeable in the same watch.

Similarly, the Laws of the Universal System are not interchangeable in one universe, and the relationship between cause and effect is part of one order of placing, for all the systems of universes gravitating in the infinite. The observations we have made in the Higher Worlds allow us to understand more clearly the mechanism of consciousness.

Each world, each degree of magnetic concentration in the ether in which we are travelling, possesses a range and possibility of action in harmony with the elements of which it is composed.

When we project ourselves into one of these dimensions the consciousness is limited by the very nature of the matter in which it is immersed. In order to increase its powers the consciousness must function in a more rarefied magnetic atmosphere. And, as the human being can only change dimensions when he has cast off all the attractions which hold him to a lower one, it follows that each individual is given power in accordance with his evolution.

The mathematical perfection of the Universe entails an equivalent justice. The conscious being is now but a unity functioning in harmony with the principles of universal order. He thinks, he acts, with this order, in this order, and for this order, and it would be impossible for him to conceive another system for the simple reason that a more perfect one does not exist. Arrived, by dint of his own efforts, at a state of perfection which he has realized little by little, whose most distant vibrations have been experienced, it is materially and spiritually impossible for him to act in any other way. Good and evil, only differentiated by the limitations of an evolving universe, no longer hold any significance. To attribute meaning to these would be a weakness of judgment, as the human being having lived in and appreciated all the variations of the one.and the other, has chosen, in accordance with Nature, the most perfect elements which go to make up his happiness.

If we sum up the practical results of the experiment in the invisible world, thinking and acting come to one and the same kind of activity. A kind of perfect intuition allows man to realize the universality of his powers and his range of action. By instinct he feels that at the least desire, at the most feeble attraction, at the very shade of thought, the whole of his psychological faculties will set to work as one. At one and the same instant he has understood, weighed, meditated on, and acted without the collective whole of these functions hindering in the least his confident serenity, indicative of universal wisdom.

So soon as we succeed in penetrating consciously

into the different dimensions of the higher worlds, we bring away with us a greater stability in the lower worlds.

This fact which I eventually noted after several years of experience, is very important. At the beginning of our experiments we do not notice at all clearly the characteristics peculiar to each dimension. A certain apprenticeship has to be served, for which none other but oneself is of any use whatsoever. We are ignorant of what we can or should do. We tend to hesitate, let ourselves be easily baulked by all kinds of obstacles.

Once we have obtained a consciousness of life in the higher dimensions, we no longer proceed so tentatively; a displeasing shape being created in front of us is no longer intimidating. We go straight to the goal and act with far more definiteness, and certainty, on any plane on which we find ourselves.

The progressive ability which we develop and put into practice, harmonizing more with the essence of phenomena, has, as its immediate result, the obligatory selection of thoughts such as we use on earth. We deduce from this that for harmony to exist between the conscious being and the higher worlds, a series of definitely positive ideas becomes necessary. And, this observation, born of experience, sums up all morality, terrestrial and supra-terrestrial.

There is no doubt that a moral principle does exist. It becomes one with our consciousness, and combines with the ever-moving ether in which we exercise our powers.

The true morality of evolution might be expressed as having none but positive ideas, positive desires, the performance of none but positive acts, and being surrounded by positive affections.

To become positive towards ourselves, to be positive with regard to the people around us all in accordance with the facts of life and environment, sums up the finest way to live in the higher dimensions of the ether.

To be positive means that we must bring into harmony the body of moving atoms which we are using for our supra-terrestrial journeys, and the pure "Energy" of the fundamental matter.

This way of living is in direct relationship with the very nature of ether. As the material aspect of our true existence represents the negative side of evolution, by freeing ourselves from the attractions which tie us down to earth we cannot fail to evolve. In order to concentrate the positive aspect of vibrations in ourselves we have only to live a life of personal desirelessness, without self-centred aims. In acting for the general usefulness, in a completely detached manner, we do not attract to ourselves the downward energy, expressing matter. We must, then, become generators of energy. In drawing the personality away from the limiting influence of personal acts, we avoid the law of reincarnation with all its consequences.

Without becoming entirely social victims, each one of us can act according to this teaching as far as possible. It seems to me to be within the reach of all to refrain from being egotistical or vain as far as may be, and to remain simple of heart in all circumstances. The law of evolution does not call for more.

At the beginning of my experiments I noticed,

to my own cost, the effects of negative thoughts in those worlds where such things cannot live.

One day, I found myself on a fairly high plane of consciousness, carrying on a pleasant conversation with some friends. We had, for the occasion, created the image of a drawing-room in which we were all comfortably seated. Without being aware of it I used, whilst speaking, an unfortunate phrase. I had barely finished speaking when I felt a shock, followed by a giddy descent which brought me back into my physical body. The impulse had been so sudden, and I was so unprepared for it, that I remained stunned for a moment, looking around me with wide-open eyes and wondering whatever could have been the cause of such a fall. I took note of the various details of the experiment and, later on, understood that each thought is, in itself, a vibrationary world, in the selection of which greater care must be taken the further one penetrates into the pure "Energy" aspect of matter.

In practice, the images and ideas sent forth by thought must always express some quality, never a fault. All ideas relating to money or fortune must disappear. All thoughts of vanity and egotism must be avoided. All pictures which have any idea of evil, or hatred, all malevolent thoughts must be forgotten.

Remember these conditions. They are indispensable in the higher regions. They might be conceived as a mechanical necessity of the universe.

It also happened, during another experiment, that I wished to find out the effect of prayer in the Invisible. That day I used the words of the Paternoster. When I thought of the words "Deliver us from evil" I felt such a loss of strength, was so overcome, that I was forced immediately to return to earth. This expression held a negative idea. What I should have said was: "Strengthen us in good," so that vibrations of a similar nature to my words might have been created.

The experience of projection in the different dimensions of space allows us to infer with absolute certainty the existence of an order of Principles in action throughout the universe. The human consciousness is enriched by its past experiences, of which it retains the basic harmonies. In the invisible worlds the magnetic subtleness of the movements of the matter allows us to bring all these experiences into play, without any effort, in one great synthesis of thought and action.

The evolution of this consciousness consists in drawing nearer to the "constants" of the Universal Order, in order to be capable of vibrating in harmony with It.

The potential of moving energy, which we know as human consciousness, is developed by the practice of a positive life. In order to eliminate from one's existence all those forces which sap one's energy, all discords created during successive ages, all negative acts and desires, one must become, onself, an attracting and positive centre within the universe.

In order to summarize the way of living in order to obtain the maximum development with a minimum effort, and in a practical manner, I would suggest that we must think, desire, act and love in a higher manner.

During every moment of our lives we must be

ready to bring into action the majestic powers of a higher life, and for that purpose must make use of universal attraction in its finest and highest sense.

Whatever the kind of attraction which is affecting us we must never act towards it in a negative manner. It is necessary that one be its absolute master. If it happens to be one which is personal, depreciating, wild, or hostile, we must remove its negative character; then this impulse will become our servant. And, in order to achieve this goal, the consciousness must be centred fully on the best in the universe, on principles of order, whose harmony is perceived by us under the various aspects of the Good, the Beautiful, and the True.

In seeking a disinterested Good in all things, in loving Beauty in all its forms, in wanting to know Truth stripped of all human illusions, giving to this ideal the backing of the whole of our being, without any reservations, we may be certain of being in complete agreement with the "constants" of evolution.

CHAPTER XII

THE obstacles that hinder one when exploring the more subtle worlds are fairly numerous. Whatever their power may be, remember that the essential condition required in order to conquer them is *moral purity*. Without this all other means lose their efficacy and may even become dangerous, coming back on their author.

The man or woman who sets about these experiments with a pure heart and a definite uplift of the moral consciousness is sure of success.

In my last chapter I pointed out the relationship which exists between moral laws and the mathematical nature of the fundamental matter of our universe. You should now have obtained some idea of their importance and scientific value. We are no longer concerned with the word "moral" as we have been used to understand it. Its mediæval aspect has disappeared altogether. Morality is no more than an intelligent selection of the forces favourable to our evolution, an evolution imposed by the active composition of both man and the universe. It is by moral conduct that we synchronize these worlds one with the other.

The hindrances we meet are a useful means of becoming conscious of the extent of our powers. At first we feel a certain pleasure in struggling against them. Later on, when we have become fully conscious of our mental power, we no longer attach the some importance to them. We are so sure of success that we can carry on with an ease similar to that with which, on earth, we would carry an object from one place to another. In short, when we have penetrated the other dimensions and become aware of their characteristics, self-defence is no longer necessary, as the obstacles no longer confront us.

The state of consciousness which precedes the disappearance of these hindrances is rather curious. When it is a matter of having to defend ourselves against entities existing in the invisible worlds, we conquer with regret--I might almost add, with pain. We suffer from having to defend ourselves. The feeling is similar to that experienced by a father who is forced to punish the children whom he loves.

Two kinds of obstacles are met in the invisible realms. The first of these are beings living in a lower stratum of the fundamental matter, and the second are images created by ourselves or by un-known intelligences.

To defend yourself from any of these, all you have to do is to call your guides, to raise the con-sciousness to a higher and purer level, or to make the sign of the cross.

To understand the nature of the obstacles and the means of self-defence it is essential to keep in mind the experimental definition of human existence in the invisible worlds. It cannot be too often repeated that the elements which make up the Invisible constitute the true "scheme" of evolution.

Two essential differences characterize the life of space and physical life.

(1) The principles of authority and of power are functions dependent upon the moral loftiness of the consciousness.

(2) Life in the rarefied matter of the subtle worlds necessitates a perception and a placing of the conscious "I" in the directive influences of the universal order.

Thus it is materially and spiritually impossible for beings of a lower state of evolution to live, consciously, in the higher worlds, as long as they have not harmonized their consciousness with the finer vibrations of those strata.

In the invisible realm, to change from one plane or dimension to another calls for an intrinsic alteration in one's component elements. If an individual is unable to adapt himself to that change he cannot live on a higher plane.

If a fish is taken out of water there is only one thing he can do in order to live in the open air—to die and be reborn with a different organism.

To change from one plane or dimension to another is to die; that is to say, to abandon all lower desires in order to live in a system composed of more subtle elements.

Broadly, human life on earth is nothing more than the result of our aspirations. It is enough to WILL in order never to return. If you are not ready to adapt yourself to the moral impulse of evolution and progress, if you cannot see, or sense, the directing principles of humanity and live in them and them alone, it will be quite impossible for you to exist in the matter of the higher worlds and to make conscious use of the energy of its ultra-sensitive atoms.

Therefore, the obstacles we are likely to meet in the Invisible world are the results of the inferior quality of our own aspirations, which place us provisionally at the mercy of the lower vibrations of matter and its denizens. As we centre our affections on an Ideal more in accord with the Great Fundamentals of the universe; as we strive to understand those Principles and make them into an integral part of ourselves, we suppress the other ties and sever all connections with the elements of disorder.

The gradual surrender of all egotistical tendencies and the simultaneous acquisition of moral energy are only the first steps in evolution, which must be completed by the intellectual grasp of the law of Cause and Effect.

These first few steps are, in all cases, a necessary and indispensable basis. Their mastery favours the germination and free development of the higher functions of the soul. It is for this reason that the great teachers of all time have advised and taught brotherly love, mutual tolerance, and the practice of goodness of heart.

In order to discern the qualities of the forms and beings which you encounter in the subtle worlds it is necessary to consider as an actual reality any plane upon which you may be functioning.

In order to pass from one dimension to another it is necessary to abandon some part of one's make-up; just as, at death, the physical body is left behind.

When you are on earth a prison is a real obstacle.

Project yourself, and it is nothing more than a picture through which you can pass, with ease, as if it did not exist. On the other hand, in the projected state, if an astral box closes you in, you are well and truly imprisoned. Leave the astral plane, project yourself into a higher dimension, and you then escape from the malevolent influences that are holding you back. If, instead of going higher, you are satisfied by going back to earth, then the astral prison will mark your psychic limits. Only an exodus to a higher plane can free you, or else the emission of a greater force of the same nature.

Each world, earthly or super-terrestrial, is therefore a momentary reality. In order to conquer it, we must abandon it, and seek refuge in a more powerful atmosphere.

The quality of the beings with which one comes into contact are easy to discern. The vibratory system which we are using as a body transmits the slightest influence. By the good or evil sensation experienced, it is easy to tell with what type we have to deal.

Remember, as a general rule, that in the invisible worlds the moral consciousness is all-powerful. Remember, also, that a thought is often enough to cause an entity which pleases or displeases us to appear or disappear.

CHAPTER XIII

HOW TO DISCERN THE QUALITY OF LIVING BEINGS

MANY schools of occultism regard as unavoidable obstacles of a lower order of evolution. To which special names are given.

Certainly, in the dense and noisome matter of the lower worlds are to be found types of beings upon the descriptions of which I do not think it necessary to elaborate. It will be enough if I give examples of times when I have been forced to struggle against malevolent entities.

One day I had projected myself with a definite intention of rising to higher planes. As I then had little practice, I did not know how to proceed correctly. Projection took place with ease. With my consciousness as clear as a bell, I found myself projected with perfect self-mastery. I leapt into space. The atmosphere was fairly clear. In the middle of a fine blue sky I noticed, set higher up, a house, which was surrounded by rather heavy clouds. I began to make my way towards this when I noticed that a "Being" was coming towards me. He was dressed in a cloak whose dark grey colour did not inspire confidence in me; yet, despite my mistrust, I went on my way with him. Soon I found myself in the centre of a town, being chased by men in black. Passing through the forms which were being built up around me, hiding in one house and then another, I found myself shut up in a kind of small cavern from which there was no exit. Mentally, I called for my guide. Immediately I was freed from the illusions created by these beings. All trace of houses or town had disappeared. I was in space, surrounded by about fifteen persons who were quite incapable of hiding their malevolent thoughts. My curiosity aroused, I contemplated their envious and sneering faces and made the protective sign of the cross. They staggered back slightly, but once more came forward laughing and talking foully. I made this an opportunity to try out the value of the so-called magical signs: triangles, pentagons, divine names, etc. Not only did these have no effect, but they mimicked my gestures, laughing and sneering at me all the while. They even managed to catch hold of my arm in order to stop me. The result was that I lost my temper. This was a mistake. I came hurtling back into my body, furious with rage, my teeth clenched, but luckily unharmed. A few moments later I made a second projection, but was not troubled by any further attacks of this kind.

I have learnt since that the best and most powerful protection is a thought of love, which may be symbolized by the sign of the cross.

During another experiment I was being chased by an individual whose thoughts created cubes in which he tried to shut me up. Suddenly he attacked me. I had the feeling of being kicked twice on the head. Despite the pain, I managed to free myself and take up the offensive. I destroyed his thought-forms and rose above him to a somewhat higher stratum. Still, he did his best to follow. Being unable to reach me, his powerful will took the shape of stones which it seemed that he was throwing at me. Tired of his insistence, I became aggressive and raised a huge bench over his head. . . . Luckily I stopped in time, put down my weapon, and forgave him. Immediately a strange metamorphosis took place, and I saw this entity turn into a dog.

During the ups and downs of this struggle I had never ceased from praying and, as I rose above my opponent, I could feel my energy increasing.

During such experiments it would be interesting to study the relationship existing between the birth of forms and their ensouling ideas. This would prove a real key to dreams. It would naturally be necessary to observe and note the association of ideas, of sentiments, and desires corresponding to the images created, and to consider the density of the matter where these manifested.

For example, in the above-mentioned instance, why did this bench have the rustic form; i.e. of a long thick plank propped up on two short ones? Would not the image of a revolver have been far more appropriate to the occasion?

Here is another case which I can remember quite clearly:—

I had not been feeling well for some days. Despite this I was sucked up by a whirlwind which carried me up in an unknown direction. As soon as I became aware of what was happening I tried to stand up in the magnetic stream which was carrying me away. I managed this, not without effort, when, to my surprise, I saw an individual of menacing aspect coming towards me, driving me into a corner of a cube which he had created, and by means of which he tried to hem me in. Fully conscious, and without any trace of dream experience, I felt a momentary reaction of natural fear. It was no more than a flash, and quickly dissipated. Regaining confidence, I stood where I was, folded my arms, leaned against the impassable barriers, and smilingly awaited the coming of this enemy. Without speaking or moving, I let him draw near. When he raised his arm to strike I mentally called my guides. He stopped transfixed, but retained his threatening air. At last he drew back slightly, stopped, stepped back once more, slowly at first and then more quickly, until I made him finally vanish by stretching out my arm and pointing my right index finger in his direction. Then I continued with my interrupted projection. The magnetic current once more took up its flow. The atmosphere became clearer and I saw below me green valleys, trees, rivers, and houses. I came at length to a town which I had intended to visit. When I regained my physical body I was strangely enough free from the indisposition which had been troubling me. I might add that at the time when this took place I had been training for eighteen months only.

Independent of the images and forms created by malevolent entities, the influence which surrounds these is definitely significant. Thus, in the first instance, the evil influence of the people by whom I was surrounded came to me in the form of invisible electro-magnetic waves of an extraordinary power of resistance. Though seeing nothing, I encountered a veritable wall of energy of considerable power.

This perception may be quite useful when one is dealing with intelligences who may be more advanced than oneself, but who are unbalanced by their moral inferiority.

Here is an instance. I had projected myself with the intention of contacting beings superior to our degree of civilization. I felt myself rise into a misty atmosphere. All of a sudden, without warning, I found myself standing before a Being who was seated on a kind of throne, and whose form was painted with various colours. His cold and severe appearance impressed me unfavourably. However, as he assured me that he was one of my guides, I guessed that I was mistaken and, overcoming my antipathy, tried to speak with him concerning my work on earth. Then, strangely enough, my memory suddenly failed me. When I came back to my body I deduced that Beings who are really good are in need of no other distinctive mark.

In fact, I learned later on to appreciate the sublime love of those Beings who are really of a higher order. Without form and without colour, the radiance of their aura inspires a feeling of such intense love, attracts us by a power so confident and devoted, that there are no words on earth capable of giving any idea of the power and quality of the energy which emanates from them.

CHAPTER XIV

HOW TO CONQUER ANTAGONISTIC FORCES

THE obstacles we are likely to meet in this second category are more varied and more frequent. They even imply in certain circumstances, long practice in projection.

The main aim of antagonistic forces seems to be to hinder the experimenter. They therefore produce images which try to imprison the student in space, or they attempt to sap his vitality.

The first kind are many in number: barriers, very narrow tubes, boxes, cages, and prisons, all aiming at the same result. Picture creations of insulating agents such as grease and glass are also used by these forces.

In the second instance, pointed objects are created, or mirages of rain, which draw away the student's strength and force him to return to his physical envelope.

Note that all these hindrances are produced when we leave our room in order to reach a new dimension. Also, I would remind you of an elementary precaution. Be sure, before launching your double into space, that you are really projected, and that your physical body is safely in bed.

I now propose giving a few instances which

demonstrate the above-mentioned obstacles in action. During one of my experiments, half-past two in the morning had hardly struck, when I began to feel my body becoming heavy and numb under some magnetic influence. Very soon I found myself out-side my body, in my own room, and fully conscious.

I went towards the door, intending to pass through it. I had hardly done this when a new room appeared and kept me prisoner. Making the sign of the cross, I dispelled the illusion, but immediately another room took its place, this time one with a window. In order to leave this room I broke the window-panes. Still under the power of the mysterious influence, the glass broke into sharp points. As it was not the first time that such a thing had happened I decided to risk it and tried to squeeze my way past the jagged edges guarding this opening. I then experienced a feeling which is rather hard to define. I was neither cut nor scratched. I felt only a strange discomfort which drew away my strength, as if it had been held in a reservoir from which it was rapidly being emptied. I had to return to my body, not having enough energy to go on.

I began a second experiment. The same obstacles came up again, with this difference, that the cubic space in which I was shut up had neither door nor window. I made my invocation and then, pointing the index and middle fingers of my right hand, exteriorized my thoughts by making the sign of the cross. The walls of my prison began to crumble and break down, only, however, to rebuild themselves as before. At last, all my attempts being useless, I regained my body.

A third attempt was, at last, crowned with success. As soon as I was in my astral body I flung myself into space, without any other vision than a fine, clear atmosphere whose magnetism gave me a very pleasant feeling. Soon I had the impression of being in the midst of heavy clouds like white cumuli. I went upward at an angle in this cloudy atmosphere and, later on, horizontally. Passing by on my upward journey I saw various study groups being held in odd corners of space. I would stop for a little while at each one, take some part in the discussions, then would go on further in this "tour of inspection." After having passed a group of children, who, it seemed to me, could have benefited by a little more discipline, I arrived at a meeting presided over by three Beings who were dressed in golden cloaks. After having shaken hands with them I sat down and listened to the lecture they were delivering. After the meeting we talked together. I could feel their brotherly friendship with the same happiness as is experienced when well-loved people are found after many years of absence. We then prayed together, and I finished my astral journey by paying a series of visits on earth.

These study-groups represent one of the many aspects of life in Space.

Sometimes obstacles crop up during a projection in the same manner as occurred during the following experiment. I was wandering about a town built in the ether when, arriving at a certain spot, I saw, to my great surprise, that the streets were closing up in front of me. Soon I found myself in a sort of tube shut up at both ends. Immediately I invoked my guides. The tube then allowed me to pass through, but again I found myself held prisoner, in a cubic space in which there was a window. The panes of this window had a circular opening protected by pointed glass in the shape of a star. Despite these points I managed to pass through, and although I lost a good deal of energy, I was not so exhausted as to be unable to finish my experiment before returning to earth.

Another time, I was stopped, during a projection, by iron spikes fixed in a board which was placed inside a wall through which I was trying to pass.

During another experiment, it had been hard work getting out of the body. In the projected state my double became the victim of a very disagreeable rotary movement. However, despite this, I travelled hundreds of miles, intending to visit one of my friends living on earth, when a grating suddenly sprang up before me. By an effort of will I forced it to disappear and continued my journey. Already I was near my goal. I could actually feel the magnetic aura of the person in question, when I had the very definite impression of being attracted by two opposing forces. One was pushing me towards my goal, the other was pulling me back. Despite my efforts, I had to yield to the second force and come back to my body. Contrary to my usual experience I was drenched with perspiration and felt a violent pain at the top of my head.

Another day, after having projected my astral body in the room where I lay, I rose perpendicularly into space. Suddenly a series of thatched roofs came in my way, doing their best to stop this ascent. Aided by prayer, I managed to see daylight and carry on my studies in good conditions.

In other cases I have been stopped from going further by a kind of grease which would suddenly impregnate all the objects around me at whatever spot I visited.

On the other hand, I was once helped by a blade of steel which had been given to me by friends on the other side.

The phenomenon of rain is a fairly frequent obstacle. As soon as I am out of my body I sometimes find myself under a dark and menacing sky. If I go forward it starts raining. Then my strength seems to ebb away, and I find it necessary to return to earth. On some occasions this space seems to be lit by magnificent sunlight. A gentle warmth fills the atmosphere. Flooded with happiness by this vivifying magnetism I have plunged joyfully into its depths when, without warning, the sky darkens and it begins to rain. The impression on the consciousness is analogous. Annoyed at first, then anxious, one's impression becomes definitely bad. The astral body seems to dissolve under the influence of this darkening picture, and it becomes necessary to return to earth in order to gather a new stock of energy.

Only after ten years' experimenting have I been able to conquer this important obstacle. The day on which I realized this I was wandering in my astral body over a sea lit up by a kind of sunlight with the same characteristics as the one I have just mentioned. It was with a feeling of deep pleasure that I travelled over these moving plains of water when, suddenly, the sky darkened. Calm up to that moment, the sea now grew rough. Heavy black clouds began to collect. Soon it began to rain, lightning flashed, to the accompaniment of terrible thunder, and a tempest was let loose. I did not feel the least uneasiness and, from the rock on which I had landed, I flew through this tempest with the same serenity and well-being as when the ocean had been sunlit.

To sum up, I would suggest that, with constant and sustained moral energy, it is possible, given some experience, to overcome all obstacles.

Before finishing this subject, it might be worth mentioning a few unpleasant things which may happen to the physical body. I myself have never suffered anything very serious, which shows, better than any amount of hypothesis, the value of my methods.

Once I had trouble with an unreasonable fear. As I opened my eyes it was quite impossible for me to make the least movement. My body was paralysed. The beating of my heart was almost imperceptible and my limbs would not obey my will. So I took the line of least resistance and went to sleep. After a few hours I awakened, tired, aching all over, and feeling as if I had been beaten with a stick. This made me meditate on the state of those unfortunate people who are buried alive. I imagined them lying in their graves, fully conscious of all that is going on, yet unable to move or cry out.

The following instance is rather unusual. During the day I had been overcome with a lassitude so profound that I was forced to go to bed. I slept for six hours and awakened in an apparently normal state. As soon as I had risen, I felt extraordinarily light. I felt as if I were walking on air and my legs were moving far too quickly.

At first this amused me. I had the impression of being in an intermediary condition between earth and a less material substance, and this form of disequilibrium was new to me. At last, I remembered my social obligations and, walking down into the street, boarded a tram. This semi-exteriorization had not come to an end, though, and it somewhat diminished my nervous sensitivity. It therefore happened that, on stepping off the tram, I was nearly run over. No longer having a full control over my body, I still had the feeling of walking on air. On stepping off the tram it seemed as if a chasm were opening at my feet, and I reacted violently in order to keep my balance. All this took scarcely a second. Anyone looking on would only have seen me take a few steps faster than was necessary. I did not fall, but the vividness of the impressions which I experienced in so minute a fraction of time is beyond imagination. At all events, I do not consider that such states of spontaneous levitation are to be encouraged.

CHAPTER XV

WE distinguish all kinds of dreams, visions, and true astral projections, in the same way as, on earth, we differentiate between conscious and unconscious actions.

Whether the dream be caused by one of many physical sensations, by memory of past experiences, by symbolic visions, or by a simultaneous glance into many dimensions, it is impossible to mistake it for projection.

On waking, people often feel as if they have been flying over landscapes, or carried through space by some means or another. These cases are too uncertain to warrant confidence.

In order to become free of the stupidity of the teachings which shackle us to our material being we must have something more than "nearly." In order to unmask the charlatans who exploit the idea of survival in one form or another, we must have definite facts, not semi-lucid experiences.

We must work in absolute control of our psychological faculties, being fully aware of the conditions under which we are experimenting, and with vivid and full understanding of the dual state in which we find ourselves. Every attempt which fails to comply with these conditions should be ruthlessly discarded. In my experiments I have noted only one exception, which, however, goes to confirm the rule.

In my dream I was crossing a large room, in which several people were gathered, when I saw a pure white dove fly down obliquely and alight on my forehead. Immediately I found myself in a state of conscious projection, and profited by the occasion to go and visit some friends.

It is impossible to imagine the marvellous reality which lies hidden under the simplicity of this tale. Without being confused, my vision was, however, somewhat passive. However light it might be, there was a sort of veil over my dream. But, as soon as the dove had touched me, the transformation was instantaneous. As if under a magic spell I suddenly became as clear-headed as in the best moments of my physical life. This awakening of the conscious personality happens in a clear, lucid manner, with immediate memory of all the facts, past, present, and to come, in which we are interested. Whilst this was happening I was fully conscious of all the work I had done with regard to astral projection, of the presence of my sleeping body, and of the exteriorization of my double, at the same time as I was working out how best to use my momentary powers. No expression can define the feeling of joy of being free in space, all the time knowing that we are fully alive on earth. Great is the happiness at being able to act as we wish, to go where we will, without having to consider our material necessities.

Truly, if everyone could become conscious of this state, how much pain would be avoided, from how many worries of all kinds would man free himself. How furiously he would work to break his egotistical attachments, and to return no more to a body which, however beautiful it may be, is a sheer dead weight.

It is unnecessary for me to give instances of dreams, or prophetic, symbolic or warning visions, which I have experienced. Everyone knows such cases, either personally or among his friends. My only wish is to give you the means of selecting from among your dreams and thereby to obtain interesting information on the past, the present, and the future of questions whose solution you may be seeking.

.   .   .   .   .

Granting the progressive density of the matter of the invisible worlds, and the possibility of being able to bring about harmonies between our own system and that of another plane with which we may wish to communicate, the relationships between the visible and the invisible are quite easy to gauge.

The greatest difficulty is to avoid the disturbances brought about by the unconscious or the lower consciousness. Still, this inconvenience is our own fault. We have created it ourselves by the attractions we give out every second by means of our desires, thoughts, motives, and sentiments.

If we wish to communicate with other dimensions and obtain useful information, it is essential to start by creating a condition of harmony so as to select suitable wave-lengths only.

We are therefore still within the same circle and are forced to return to the conditions already expressed: physical, psychological and psychical hygiene. The more you concentrate your motives, desires, and thoughts on a Noble Ideal, the less you will be disturbed by unwanted wave-lengths.

It is therefore necessary to get rid of the old Adam; that is, patiently eliminate all the mistakes, the antitheses, the contradictions of the manners and customs of our civilization, and build on new ground the higher being, who will put you in touch with regions of a kindred nature.

Experience has shown us that the human being is a consciousness capable of living in extremely subtle matter, in which he has access to the energy which underlies phenomena.

In order that he may keep his equilibrium in this superfine matter it is sufficient to build up a system of oscillating energy, capable of synchronizing with the vibration of the higher planes, in order that the consciousness may discern their characteristics.

The above remarks are absolutely essential. Whatever may be the world in which we are living, whatever the nature of the energy being used where we travel, in order to appreciate the nature of a vibration we must have practical experience of its effects. Only experience in a world lower than the one in which we are creates in our system of harmonies potentialities which allow us, in the best degree, to differentiate between the causes and effects through which we have lived.

On this earth, not everybody is capable of appreciating the difference between the atmosphere of a dance hall and that of a church, all the more so in dealing with those finer vibratory states appertaining to the essence of the phenomenal world.

In order to understand the true life of the soul on earth and in the Invisible, in order to form a valid judgment on the conscious and unconscious manifestations of the waking and sleeping states, it is essential to realize our place in the universe.

As we have already said, we are a centre of radio-active matter, capable of radiating energy and of perceiving vibrations which give us information on the quality and reason for phenomena. In order to make accurate observations on these, in order to compare them one with another, and to deduce rational conclusions, we must first have appreciated their effects on those planes where they come into being.

These effects are of two kinds: good and evil. These qualities are decided by the density and synchronization of our own centre of energy in relationship to the material constitution of the universe. Good and evil, happiness and sorrow, are merely results due to the intimate inter-relationships existing between man and the universe. These are relationships which are built up between the inherent energy of man and the inherent energy of the universe. The universe being invariable in its relationship of cause and effect it is up to us to alter the type of attractions which belong to our centre of energy.

Everyone on earth has seen the formidable mass of suffering brought about by the chase after personal satisfaction, by evil doing, by jealousy, and by the intolerance of men towards one another. This way, therefore, is not in harmony with the types of energy in which we wish to live. Suffering indicates lack of balance, disagreement, an inharmonious relationship between man and the universe.

The conditions favourable to the happiness sought after by the human being demand the opposite path: the application of true moral law, root cause of all our experiences and their observation.

The mechanism of the relationship between man and the universe manifests in the following manner, and thereby decides the scientific basis of true moral law.

.   .   .   .

The human being has reflections acting in three main worlds by reason of his deeds, his desires, and his thoughts. According to the intensity with which he travels, concentrates his motives for action, towards the world of thought, so do these three centres of observation, these three sensory machines, take on importance. And, in the higher worlds, to think, to wish, and to act, are inseparable from one another. They melt into one faculty, responsive to the least influence, whether it comes from outside or from within ourselves.

This synthesis and speed call, therefore, for a certain choice in our ways of thinking and acting. Were it possible to reach these different dimensions and to live in their substance without having to make a mechanical selection in the direction of the forces which we bring into action, the order would not be universal.

Therefore, every time you think, or desire, or act under any influence whatever, you actuate a part of the ether whose waves will be directed towards the point which you have assigned to them. At the same time you have created in the ether a "line of least resistance" which will favour your efforts in the chosen direction. This magnetic path is a canal along which all vibrations of a similar nature will flow. If you have thought of yourself, if your aim is personal profit, if you have been moved by greed and with the sole aim of obtaining one advantage or another, this is what happens: The electronic particles of the ether which are set in motion, after having passed a portion of their energy in the desired direction, will return to you. The magnetic field thus formed will attract, by affinity, all other systems of a similar nature. Soon a veritable world will gravitate about you, attracting by sympathy all sorts of living entities of a similar quality. You are now bound to a particular system of energy, the nature of which will force you to experience the same type of attraction over and over again. For you it is easier to give way to these attractions than to create new ones. To destroy them means real suffering. We all know the power of habit and of the sweetness of obeying its call. Having no better reason for changing your mode of existence you go on living in this way your whole life through. After death, the subtle body in which you find yourself will be placed in an atmosphere having such characteristics as harmonize with its composition, and will be in the company of living beings possessed of similar tendencies.

Observation of joys experienced by the consciousness in earth-life substantiates the emptiness, the void, and the heartbreak of the conditions produced by sensual pleasures.

Observation of facts in the Invisible confirm this. In proportion to one's descent into the world of sensual attractions so do our sensations become more material. The more condensed atmosphere seems thicker. The reduction in the speed of its atoms makes it seem darker, and we experience a definite impression of stifling.

Intellectual pleasures, the healthy joy of duty well done, the conscious exercise of the finer faculties of the soul, the satisfaction of having made ourselves of use, of having contributed something towards the work of peace, of union, and of having mitigated pain, produces, on the contrary, a lasting happiness which gives the soul new strength and a higher type of energy.

Experience of the reality of the invisible planes allows us now to understand this phenomenon. All efforts thus directed put us in touch with worlds where energy radiates far more powerfully with the expenditure of a smaller amount. It is therefore quite natural that this super-activity should communicate itself to our earthly personality.

Writing from experience, the atmosphere of the invisible worlds becomes finer in proportion as we free ourselves from sensual satisfactions. The general discomfort which we experience in the lower worlds no longer exists. We are now living in a state of rest, in a state of well-being which increases until it becomes pure joy, and happiness born of perfect serenity, wholly beyond the power of my pen to describe.

Matter has followed the same evolutionary process. From the absolute darkness of the lower worlds a slight luminosity manifests and begins to increase. This clarity, which might be compared to the dawn, is at first a sort of greyish mist. Then the opacity begins to disperse, the grey becomes less dark, the mist less heavy. Lastly, this clarity intensifies, and becomes comparable to our sun at noon. Of an equal intensity at every point, this light is felt as a gentle and vivifying warmth.

In order to live in such an atmosphere, experience has shown that we must first rid ourselves of sensual attractions, then of the desire for personal satisfaction, and lastly of all material motives. This does not mean that we should live as hermits, in ascetism and seclusion. Our physical being has needs which it would be dangerous to ignore. We must not make the pretext of harmonizing ourselves with the higher worlds a means of disharmonizing ourselves with this one. It is quite feasible to live without excesses, using the material satisfactions of this world, and yet at the same time to evolve. All that is required is that we do not make these the main object of our lives and become attached to them unduly. I repeat, the calls of our material nature must merely be kept within limits. I succeeded in my experiments whilst living like anyone else, in the midst of my daily work, and without following any special regimen. When I state that ascetism is not essential I have experimental proof of it.

To sum up, the work consists of a progressive decentralization of the personality, of the isolated "I," to make it aware of the multiplicity of causes upon which it is possible to act.

To arrive at this end we must centre our attention on higher things than material pleasures. By dint of practice our concentration gradually rises from the material to the spiritual. Then, one day, it happens that we realize that our only satisfaction is to be found in the eternal principles of life.

It is interesting to note that, in this evolutionary work, the need for effort grows less, and the joy more profound in proportion to the perfecting of our system in harmony with the universal law.

The most simple way for all people is to direct their thoughts, their desires, and motives less and less on themselves. You should now realize that there is nothing mysterious in the choice of a noble ideal. It is an embodiment of the directing idea, guiding the uninitiated into this system of perfection.

Simultaneously with the diminution of self-centred interests, we should direct our minds more and more towards the beauties of life. Ignore its defects and ugliness. Always see the good side of things, and struggle with all your might to destroy whatever evil you may meet.

This conduct, which is indispensable to anyone who wishes to come into contact with the invisible planes without loss of balance and the development of psychic folly, is within the reach of everybody as part of ordinary daily life. The smallest facts of existence may serve as rungs to help us surmount our miseries. We can make use of the most insignificant details in order to develop our energy in the way of unfolding the higher consciousness.

This is the rationale of the method. The

energy which you put into movement in the substances of the invisible planes follows blindly the direction you give it, until, one day, it returns and concentrates in you.

Now you proceed to decentralize your affections, placing them on a point other than yourself. The vibrations of the ether will move towards the new goal. If this is a noble ideal, the animated atoms of the world in which you have placed it will create a body into which will be drawn all elements of equal value. Weak at first, its vibrating energy will increase rapidly. As you give more and more of the best that you have in you to this noble ideal, this nucleus of energy will metaphorically grow like a snowball and produce a well-defined system into which it will be easy for you to plunge, leaving the old state, without regret, to its fate.

By struggling against evil by means of moral perfection, by trying to see the usefulness of all things, by realizing the charm, the poetry, the beauty of nature, you will learn to love life for its own sake. In seeking to find beauty in its various guises, and then in its expression, you will soon learn to love that beauty itself rather than its forms. In seeking out that which binds together your deeds, desires, thoughts, and affections, you learn to love good for its own sake. This is the true path of the initiate. The secret of life is contained in this mechanism, and lies within the reach of all.

In proportion to your realization of the good and the beautiful so do you find your way towards the true source of freedom and happiness. By your efforts you learn to live in constant harmony, and you soon have no wish for anything else. On that day you will be very near to true perfection.   For a long time you will have been able to communicate with these wonderful worlds into which we penetrate, and the domain of dreams will hold no further secrets for you.

CHAPTER XVI

SOME REMARKS ON THE MECHANISM OF INTUITION AND INSPIRATION

THE development of these studies has allowed me to notice certain characteristics concerning the different means by which we can get in touch with the invisible worlds.

In order to discuss these phenomena in a satisfactory manner it is best to begin by regarding the human being as a wireless station, capable of acting both as transmitter and receiver. The selection of the wave-lengths that we wish to transmit, or receive, calls for the use of elementary psychical exercises.

In order to bring one's psychical being into harmony with the higher worlds we must orient our thoughts in the direction of moral goodness. I am assuming that we are willing to proceed in an orderly and methodical manner. It is the only way of obtaining rational results.

The different expressions which have so far been used fail to define accurately the present category of phenomena. The word "clairvoyance" is not exact. It is possible to contact the invisible planes without being clairvoyant. Neither is the word "medium" a proper one. We are in no way intermediaries, but conscious operators. Although

I am not in favour of creating new definitions, I nevertheless find it useful to define all psychical procedure having as its aim contact with the invisible planes, as "Transconscious," "trans" being a Latin preposition which signifies the passage from one place or state to another. We shall therefore speak of transconscious transmission or reception. This word gives the idea of an act through the consciousness, and this, in fact, is the first rule to follow. Every phenomenon which has as its aim establishment of communication with other worlds should be conscious. The student must be allowed full freedom of mind. He ought to be able to note calmly, coolly, and precisely the smallest details. His observations should be independent, as if it were another person working, and he must not allow himself to become absorbed to any extent. Needless to say, he must be in good health physically and psychically, the mind free from worry and, after a little practice, he should realize the fullest lucidity and freedom of will which it is possible to obtain.

The scheme and the experimental conditions in every case are the same as for personal projection. All that is altered is the directive influence of thought.

It is possible to study the phenomenon of telepathy on this basis. In order to succeed in these experiments it is above all necessary that the transmitter and receiver should work together on the day and at the time agreed upon. On no account should these be changed. Both experimenters establish harmony between them by reciprocal thoughts of friendship. The one who is acting as receiver makes his mind blank, and silently observes the vibrations which come to him. These vibrations may present themselves in the guise of pictures, of sounds, or of thoughts. Distance is of no importance and has no influence on the production of the phenomenon. At the beginning, the transmitter must avoid sending complicated phrases. He ought to formulate his thought in one word, sending it outwards as strongly as he can. He should imagine that he is shouting into the ear of his recipient, or that the letters are being engraved in the ether, or are producing a powerful sound, and so on. I once received thoughts from a distance of ten thousand miles as loudly as if someone had shouted them in my ear. Surprised at such a result, I sprang up to see who was standing beside me. This reflex action shows now necessary it is to undertake serious training.

Psychic healing, practised in this way, gives results which seem miraculous to the uninitiated. In my opinion, if you wish to become fully conscious of your powers, the best training you could have is to practise mental healing. I would advise you to treat your patient without his knowledge. Do not let the factor of distance disturb you. The results are exactly the same if you are separated by one mile or by several thousands of miles. Preferably treat your patient when he is in bed or asleep. No illness can resist this treatment, which is the most powerful known up to the present day, unless the disease be of Karmic origin. I have also noticed that the treatment should never be stopped abruptly, but diminished gradually.

It is equally possible, by means of mental medicine, to treat oneself successfully. We can recover our strength almost instantaneously, or inhibit the evil effects due to other persons or events, and in fact, change the conditions of life. I repeat, the neutralization of the vibrations produced by our general way of living is the only limiting factor to these powers. It depends entirely on ourselves to what pitch we bring these according to our will to sacrifice the lesser for the greater things. The moral conduct which I have already pointed out is therefore an absolute necessity.

As the same mechanism controls the conscious transmission of thought we may establish contact with every degree of the universal substance, from its aspect of crude matter up to that of pure energy.

The response varies in nature. Usually it comes in the form of a dream, in which a symbolic picture allows us to adapt it to our particular character and temperament.

Should you practise in the morning, reception may take place by vision or by intuition.

Vision may manifest itself in an inanimate fashion, such as a landscape projected as by a magic lantern; or a scene may be enacted, as in a cinema film. In the latter case it may even happen that you will be taking a more or less active part in the proceedings.

We now come to intuition, which I would call "Reception without form."

Although they are first cousins, we must not confound intuition with inspiration.

Intuition does not permit of reasoning, however instantaneous. It is the formless reception of vibrations, varying from pure intuition to the clairaudient word. It is an idea, or a series of ideas, which come, at first in a confused manner, then more and more clearly until one seems to hear as well as if a friend were speaking into one's ears. Sometimes the idea comes and goes with the speed of a lightning flash. On other occasions it seems as if we were perceiving the idea through an obstacle.

The development of intuition takes place in the same way as for the other processes of communication. Lying down in calm and silence we concentrate our minds on the problem to be solved, and do our best to drive away all thought from the field of consciousness. So soon as an idea, or series of ideas, comes clearly to the mind, note it immediately.

If we consider intuition as the beginning of a mental correspondence between ourselves and the other dimensions of space, it is then possible to say that inspiration represents its stabilization and completion. In intuition we listen, and catch vibrations as they pass. In inspiration, on the other hand, it is not necessary to listen, because all the intellectual faculties are at a maximum of activity. It is no longer a case of mental communication, but you yourself who draw deductions, with incomparable ease. Inspiration, therefore, is an excellent working method which becomes more and more stabilized by training, and becomes a regular method of mental intercourse with the Invisible.

In order to put it into practice we must start by forming the habit of working regularly, on fixed days and at a definite time. It is also advisable mentally to invoke friendly Powers, to burn salt mixed with incense, all of which help in purifying the psychic atmosphere of the room set apart for working, and in harmonizing one's psychical vibrations.

Let us suppose we wish to delve deeply into a subject by logical analysis and synthesis. In order to judge freely and to avoid falling into ordinary errors, we must first of all define exactly the subject to be studied. Then we must become acquainted with the latest investigations in the subject. Lastly, by an effort of will, we must drive all this information from the mind, and set to work as if we knew nothing whatever about the matter to be studied.

It is by following such a scheme in the organization of our studies that inspiration will come.

At first we do not take exact account of the phenomenon. During a moment when all our thoughts are deeply concentrated on our work, a sudden flood of ideas will surge through the mind. The pen cannot write quickly enough. Under the sway of this panorama of thoughts we can write, meditate, reason, and deduce with marvellous ease. After having written a number of pages in which we believe we have discovered the solution of the problem, we are brought up short by some question which seems to be bristling with obstacles. We stop working, worried by this new aspect of the subject about which we had not dreamed. The next time, having worked on this new idea, we start work once more. The same clear insight is manifested, bringing in its train the joy of seeing new points of view, until yet another difficulty intervenes. This one always seems worse than the other. We ask ourselves whether it is reasonable to carry on with this method. At last we try again, and sufficiently interesting results reward us for the efforts we have made.

Under the influence of concentration of thought,

we focus our consciousness on the purely mental plane, which gives rise to new associations of ideas. Such is the mechanism of the phenomenon.

Several years of training are needed before inspiration becomes a regular working method. Numerous obstacles hinder its development : bad physical or psychological conditions, the temperature or humidity of the atmosphere, education, home life, general surroundings, daily impulses and ways of thinking, all play a part in helping or hindering the development of this new faculty.

Thus, on certain days we no sooner sit down to our work than we come under the spell of this higher understanding. Everything seems childishly simple. And this state seems so normal that it is as if it had always existed and would now last for ever.

Then, if at that moment we bring our attention to bear on the phenomenon itself, in order to discover its rationale, everything stops immediately and we find ourselves unable to put two ideas together.

At other times, on the contrary, we feel in excellent form. We sit down at our desk quite sure that we shall obtain extraordinary light on the work in hand. An hour goes by, two hours, without the slightest results. Even if we carry on for from four to five hours nothing will happen. The mind seems covered with an impenetrable veil and we give up in a state of bad temper and dissatisfaction.

The periods of work carried out under the influence of inspiration are marked by a feeling of peace, of joy, and of confidence which stays with us the whole day.

The "atmosphere" which surrounds us at such times varies with the subject we are studying. When we are dealing with questions relating to the inter-correlation of our microcosm and the Absolute, then tears will spring unbeckoned to our eyes, and it is with indescribable joy that we arrive at deeper understandings.

This method of working must not be mistaken for ecstasy. In this inspirational condition we remain fully conscious. But the ideas which we are handling are impregnated with such a marvellous atmosphere that the vibrations, in spite of oneself, act on our emotions. If our desire to know the ultimate word, the cause of all things, has been pushed far enough, we shall find ourselves trembling, and tremendous shudders, as from a strong shock, will run up our body, from feet to head.

In this state we lose all sense of time. After several hours of steady work it seems as if we had only been at it for a few minutes, and if someone interrupts, we seem to be holding our breath as if falling from a great height.

The study of the relations between geometric figures and numbers calls for more difficult training. At first it is impossible to give all the time we could to this work, as the mind grows dizzy and this mad whirl hinders the work. Broadly speaking, inspiration is easier to develop on moral and philosophic matters than on metaphysics, which call for a far deeper concentration of thought.

Inspiration may prove very tiring, and this manifests itself by a feeling of emptiness. The head seems hollow, and the body aches all over as a result of the nervous expenditure.

These undesirable sensations which accompany inspiration will disappear in time. The phenomenon is transformed into a lasting faculty, neither more nor less obvious than those we already possess. We only work in a more regular manner, without sudden spurts, and in a state of profound peace above either joy or depression, in the knowledge that we are doing something useful.

In other to develop and regulate the exercise of this faculty we may come to the following conclusions:

(1) That it is wise to choose questions bearing on morality, philosophy, and metaphysics, whose development will help the general well-being of mankind.

(2) We should try to analyse our subject calmly, beginning our work over and over again until we arrive at results which are both logical and rational.

(3) We should always act in harmony with the highest ideas that we are capable of understanding, and should pay attention both to physical and mental hygiene.

CHAPTER XVII

RELATIVE VALUES OF THE TEACHINGS AND METHODS
FOR DEVELOPING PERFECTION USED IN THE
INVISIBLE PLANES

THE metamorphosis of inspiration into a faculty which is balanced with the others, permits its possessor to come into touch with the higher planes at any time of the day, and amidst his ordinary occupations. This brings me to a point where it is necessary to detail the nature of the information we receive from the other side of life. Many persons believe that the ability to contact the state beyond the veil, or to project oneself consciously, are enough to teach us the laws of the universe. This is a mistake: they merely augment the "sum of probabilities."

The real teaching of those whom we call Guides or Masters, who are brought to us by our love, is more rational than we imagine. I can speak of this from personal experience.

It is only after long years of meditation when, from one deduction to another, we have been able to schematize the laws of the universe in a general basic order, that we realize the difficulty, we might even say the impossibility, of expressing the principle under one heading. Human consciousness works by stages. Its development calls for an intellectual perception of the connections between cause and effect and the evolutionary value of the elements we may be contacting.

Let me point out, though, once for all, that an intellectual person is not necessarily conscious in the full meaning of the word. In order to be truly conscious, it is not enough merely to observe the technical relationships of experience, but also the relationships of the universal to the particular, in regard to the application of this experience to moral utility, without which no evolution is possible.

The evolution of consciousness cannot be compared to memory which becomes enriched by a greater store of material. On the contrary, consciousness is a central focusing of all the faculties in a new synthetic unity, giving the impression of greater freedom. By analogy, consciousness expands like the horizon of the observer as he mounts further and further from the ground. Each new stage of consciousness synthesises the others into a superior state which is the key to the one which preceded it, and so on, until we attain the First Cause.

In such circumstances it would be stupid to preconceive one and the same instruction for everybody. The method followed by the Higher Intelligences is to impart knowledge according to the mentality and temperament of each student. He is guided in his best path, his eyes are opened to conceptions of which he was ignorant, and he is taught to observe, correlate, deduce, and construct new conceptions for himself.

The details of personal contact with these Intelligences does not, therefore, apply to all, but vary according to the evolution and development of the faculties of the student. The effect of such teaching is to complete, in a useful manner, what the student has already learned, and to prepare the consciousness for a development which is both "wider" and much "deeper." These teachings are beyond price for those who receive them. They allow a maximum capacity to be obtained by the student with a corresponding minimum output of effort. They enable the student to maintain his mental balance during the study of the energy which he is handling. This remark is worthy of consideration. Radiating around the same universal order, drawing each time a little nearer to the core of this cosmic system, they lead the student, little by little, to a consciousness of the universal method. The exact manner in which these teachings are distributed is superior to any modern method, as incomparable results are obtained without appreciable effort.

Daily communication with the higher worlds is a condition which occurs, after a certain time, without special preparation. The mere direction of our thoughts towards our Guides places the consciousness within the magnetic aura of the corresponding dimension. The affection held in that thought will free one's surroundings from hindering influences and all that has to be done is to take careful note of the answers obtained in order to draw logical conclusions from them.

I repeat, these instructions are not dogmatic

revelations. There is nothing supernatural or sensational about them. They are applicable in an exact, scientific manner, in a degree slightly beyond the student's mentality, whose consciousness is slowly raised into the formless regions belonging to the Fundamental Principles of life. As in any other study, surprises and unexpected viewpoints crop up. These new ideas often seem to destroy those that have gone before, but we see by what follows that they really complete them by sublimation. We therefore burn that which we have previously worshipped, in order soon to worship what we have burned. In reducing itself to a unity the consciousness assimilates human suffering and plays its part in arranging it. The higher it rises, the less aggressive becomes the spirit of man, and the noblest tolerance walks hand in hand with the peace of the higher worlds.

The same remarks apply to self-projection. The projection of the self on any plane of consciousness does not necessarily give it an integral understanding of that level. Before penetrating into a more active state, the consciousness must learn to make use of the elements in which it finds itself. It is only after having felt the effects, observed the resistance or the ease, respectively, with which these manifest the forms of thought, the subtle reactions of all nature, that we realize the possibilities and the limitations of whatever state we may be in. When this has been achieved we leave this world behind and travel forward into another, when it will be necessary once more to undergo the same studies as before in order to analyse the make-up of our new state. We go on in this manner, from ether to ether, becoming all the time more refined in our substance until, one day, we reach the culminating point where the human consciousness becomes united with the essence of all life and in this way understands the principles which give rise to existence.

If you will, once more, consider the nature of these invisible worlds, you will obtain a good idea of the work which has to be carried out there.

I have visited different dimensions, different planes, whilst taking a careful note of their inhabitants, human beings or otherwise, and the following are some of the observations I have made in regard to them.

Each state of density, or dimensional division of the ether, corresponds to our affinities, desires and preferences. Each one is therefore able to lead the life he wishes. As the majority of people are ignorant of the possibility of living consciously in space, they surround themselves with imaginary creations.

But what is the meaning of the expression, "imaginary creations"? For those who know no better their imagination is a reality. I would even claim that it is necessary to their state of being in the same way as our earthly creations are necessities of physical life. These latter are, in the astral world, no more than "illusions" and "images," yet to what trouble do we go in order to build them, what suffering do they not sometimes bring in their wake. It is therefore natural that each one should live in the world in which he finds himself, surrounded by forms constructed from the materials of that world. No one is likely to worry as to the nature of these materials in the next world. Everyone knows that atoms are particles of positive and negative electricity, revolving one around the other, at speeds and in orbits which can be determined, but no one seems to think deeply enough about the matter to realize that these atoms constitute a world which is quite real and not imaginary. No one thinks that this reality is quite as absolute in the next dimension as it is on earth. This fault on the part of our reasoning faculties is due to our ignorance of the manifestations of life in other realms of space.

The tangible, conscious, and sensory reality of the world in which we find ourselves is a universal law that no dogma can deny.

Apart from what I would call the world of Fundamental Principles, each state of the universal matter lends itself admirably to the creation of forms which represent the affections of each person. By comparison, these worlds are more perfect than our own. What are we seeking on earth? Apart from the necessities of life, each one has a goal in mind. The most ordinary is to be allowed to work in peace and then to save enough money to buy a small suburban villa in which to retire in modest comfort. To be one's own master, to have all the latest comforts, to travel and see the world, are fairly general ambitions, but these are already harder to realize. Beyond this come the more detached aims of the poets, artists, and scientists of all kinds and, further, the whole of humanity wants to live at peace with its fellows.

Suppose, for a moment that our earth and its inhabitants have been switched over to the next dimension. As all variations would have occurred in a proportionate manner no one would notice that there had been any change. Everyone would carry on with his work as if nothing had happened. All the same, an unusual atmosphere of peace would extend over all. Inter-relationships would become less harsh, would gradually become more pleasant. Everything would turn out as it should, each person would see his wishes realized very quickly, all without hindering anyone else. No more grumbling of any kind whatsoever. The social system would work like a watch. Almost incredible fact, politicians would live in peace, "civil servants" would be civil, journalists would tell the truth, trains would be punctual, and the ladies would no longer be jealous! In short, the Golden Age would have begun.

The perfection of the means used in the invisible planes is far greater even than that which I have suggested in this imaginary hypothesis, first of all because people are selected according to their impulses, which automatically place them in groups of similar character, further because Beings of a greater development come to their aid, so that they may organize a state of affairs adapted to their characters. This will allow them to rise to higher planes in accordance with the lucidity with which they realize the state in which they happen to be.

I once noticed, whilst I was in the astral world, a region in the ether where, after death, those people go who are neither good nor bad, and who know of nothing but their daily work, with its pleasures and difficulties. At first their material sensations persist. But, as I have just written, a devoted band shares the joy of helping these poor, half-blind people to put into operation the possibilities of the world in which they find themselves. They start by freeing them from their crudest material ties, and help them to organize a social system in which they will all be happy. In this state each one will devote himself to his work, and familiar habits: Technical work, administrative work, commerce, and scientific experiment, all carried out in a state of peace and calm in accordance with the nature of the matter in which they find themselves. Among others I noticed a group who were studying the circulation of the sap in a plant which had been specially enlarged for the purpose.

As I saw it, space had been divided into sections in which were placed people of similar affections. Everyone was happy. I watched a certain class of workmen draw their wages and contrive important economies. Had they but known it they had but to think of it to become multi-millionaires. In the life beyond, as on earth, all is relative. One can only become aware by acquired knowledge.

In this ideal town I could see the trams working without an accident ever happening. I visited several factories without noting any other difference from those on earth than a general happiness and well-being among all the workmen.

It was in the dwelling-places, created by different individuals, that I observed the most curious facts. By examining them I was able to follow the nature of the thoughts and feelings of their occupants. Some were simple, sober and in good taste, others large and luxurious. Many were furnished oddly, all the shapes corresponding with the mentalities of their creators.

In a world which was lower than this one I observed a group composed of voluptuaries and slaves to animal passion. The dwelling-place in certain cases would be no more than a stable smelling strongly of urine.

Whilst taking in the details of this organization, I pondered on the activities which were going on around me, and could not find any arguments in their favour.

To sum up, no one can develop except by the help of knowledge and affection. This is logical, rational and in accordance with the human constitution. By letting everyone have the means of putting these essentials to the best use, and to the greatest possible extent, one helps evolution.

It seems as if the different sections of this organization ended in cross-roads. These cross-roads represented concentration-points from which human beings were collected into their different categories. Quantities of streets seemed to end up there, from which one could go towards other planes by means of ladders set up in different directions. Waiting-rooms furnished with sofas covered with red velvet allowed new-comers to await their turn.

I shall not waste time by a lengthy recital of all my experiences on these planes. Thought being creative in these regions of space it becomes easy to imagine the perfection to which their organizations can develop. What is more, goodwill is always amply rewarded. Those Beings who are more advanced lead, little by little, those individuals who show the necessary desire, to a state of consciousness above that of their existing one. This allows them to change to a higher dimension and take on more perfect work.

CHAPTER XVIII

THE LIMITATIONS OF FREEWILL AND THE INFLUENCE OF WILL-POWER IN THE HIGHER WORLDS

THE knowledge of the manifestations of life in the higher worlds gives us the key to all the mystical visions of the Ancients, and we now understand the reason for their seeming contradictions.

The rational study of the atmospheres, whose density controls the radio-active power, demands above all absolute calmness of thought. In this way we can obtain impartial results. An exception to this rule holds good for those who are sufficiently advanced, as they know how to limit the manifestations of their thoughts.

In the higher planes the will is a magic wand and it is easy enough to put its instinctive tendencies to one side. It therefore interested me to know to what extent the will could be used and to know its relationships with freewill.

If it is a question of individual perfection there are no limits to its powers. Will grows, with full development, up to absolute freedom. Every person can aspire to escape from the evolutionary wheel by joining his consciousness with the fundamental principles of cosmic harmony.

If we seek for crude and vulgar satisfaction in the

lower worlds, our experiments are soon stopped by obstacles of all kinds. We become the victims of the Beings and Forces living in those dark regions of ether, and madness is generally the ultimate result. In these heavy atmospheres the mockery of its inhabitants is the dominating element. The thought-waves of the Beings who live there are transmitted in a fairly material manner. In the higher worlds thought is clear, precise, vivid and immediate, without the least sound being heard.

In the lower worlds it seems as if we hear a timbre of voice unknown on earth. Whilst being sustained it gives the impression of being reedy. The timbre is neither high nor low; it is strong, yet has no personality. Its resonance is quite different from our own and yet very distinct. As to the sensations we experience in these worlds, these are almost material.

During one experience I could just make out, through the dark atmosphere of one of these planes, a deceased person standing on the step of a staircase. The imagery had brought into being the entrance of a cave where absolute darkness reigned. I walked down a few steps, being attracted by this entity who, straightaway, embraced me. Despite the fact that I was fully conscious of my condition, and already long practised in projection, the material feeling was so strong that, in spite of myself, I opened my eyes, certain that someone had disturbed me during my experiment. I recognized my mistake immediately. It was too late and I had lost an excellent chance of making some very interesting discoveries. I could only remember the feeling of "cold" and "touch."

Also, though it is possible to pass through all the

houses in a town, as if they were not there, we must
not imagine that we can go into any man's place
against his will. If this were the case it would be a
matter of perpetual intrusion, with all sorts of
troubles ahead. What family skeletons would be
exposed! Rest assured, in the Invisible, liberty is
sacred, and the will inviolable.

Unless your feelings are in harmony with those
you draw around you, have no fear of unwelcome
visitors. Your dwelling is unbreachable and no
amateur detective can use this means to make
enquiries in your house.

In order to establish unbroken relationships with
persons living on earth, we must have very strong
ties with such individuals, who must be parents,
children, fiancés, or friends with whom we are
spiritually united.

The ties of comradeship are not always enough.
On this point I once made the following interesting
experiment.

A young man, who was my neighbour, was
interested in psychic matters, and told me that he
was eager to have proof of astral projection. I
therefore arranged that I should visit him astrally
that evening. His house was close by, and I was
familiar with its interior arrangements. Considering
that I was used to projecting myself to a distance of
hundreds of miles into an unknown house in a
strange country, without having any other guide
than my own affection, this experiment was mere
child's-play.

However, I encountered serious difficulties. At
the first attempt I was hemmed in by unknown forces
which made me cry out with pain and spoiled the

projection. The second time I was luckier, and managed to go into the room of the young man, but was quickly driven away by the unfriendly atmosphere. I hardly had the time to see him lying in bed, his face slightly luminous, and to cry out his name, as had been arranged, when I was pushed back by an unknown force. I had the idea that this energy was projected by someone called Jacques. I expressed a mental wish to see him. At once, this unknown person appeared in the form of a soldier with a fixed bayonet, menacing and insulting me. After much effort I managed, first, to disarm him, and then to send him away by making the sign of the cross. From that moment the experiment took its normal course. I returned to my body and, after having noted the details of what had happened, once more set off, very conscious of myself and wide awake. After having passed through my children's room, I crossed, in one leap, the space which separated me from our rendezvous. Arriving on the roof of my friend's house a magnetic current tried to carry me away. I resisted, and came down, perpendicularly, into the sleeper's room. I saw him lying in bed in a sort of flannel vest with his arms bare. Placing my hands on his arms, so as to make him feel my presence, I told him that I was near him, fully conscious of my dual state, and aware of everything that was happening. I returned to my body and the next day questioned the young man. All the details of the experiment were exact. A friend of his named Jacques had, in fact, left his place some days ago. So far as my visit was concerned my neighbour had not been aware of it.

Broadly speaking we can go anywhere when we are travelling, but when our thoughts have a definite object, we must allow for the freewill of others, and for the resistances due to the psychic atmosphere around the place we are visiting.

It has happened that, during my experiments, I have met resistance in the guise of black clouds emanating from the house where the person I wished to visit was living. I was able to conquer these, thanks to sympathetic vibrations emitted by furniture which had belonged to me and pieces of which were in the flat.

From all my experiments I have come to the conclusion that the will exercises, in the Invisible, power proportionate to the accuracy of our knowledge and to the disinterestedness of our motives. The separation of these two essential factors induces a lack of balance which becomes the more dangerous as the personal egotism is accentuated.

CHAPTER XIX

HOW TO DISTINGUISH BETWEEN THOUGHT-FORMS AND LIVING BEINGS

BEING granted the vast field of matter in which all types of energy find a home, and whose radio-activity ranges from a possible minimum to a possible maximum, it is easy to imagine the construction of the living forms of nature. There is not an atom, not a vibration, however feeble it may be, which is not registered in the cosmic substance.

On the side of crude matter the particles of energy occupy a minimum of space. Inertia is at its maximum, less a necessary fraction without which it could not respond to any vibration whatever. It is under the greatest compression possible without going beyond the limits of our universe. It is the extreme limit of life in the material world.

On the side of substance the speed of the atoms is distributed into space which is at its greatest extension. The infinitely small fraction of mechanical inertia which remains to these atoms corresponds in the same proportion to the energy which animates the inertia of crude matter. Energy is then reduced to its simplest expression. To go beyond this would mean that we would once more have to leap beyond the boundaries of our universe in order to contact a reality far too abstract for our consciousness to grasp. This expression of the atoms radiates to its greatest extent when the aspect of crude matter is only a point seen at the uttermost extremity of space.

These extreme aspects of the universal substance balance in a kind of reciprocal fecundation, which is none other than "life," a neutral current, capable of manifesting in all parts of the universe without upsetting the equilibrium of the system of forces which it represents.

This quadruple relationship of vital energy is the reason why it is possible for the human to leave the universe in which he has come to consciousness of his relative and absolute possibilities.

This scheme of our cosmic system will explain to you why all movements, whatever their nature, are registered in the invisible substance. As it happens they could not manifest otherwise. The attracting energy, which varies from a maximum of compression to a maximum of extension, calls for some support it finds in the universal substance whose variable proportions of pure energy and crude matter define the nature of the world in which we live.

In these conditions all the worlds are as real as one another. The least and the greatest are indispensable to the conscious differentiation which constitutes the essential part of the human being. This texture, or woof, under which the cosmic universe shows itself to the student in a state of self-projection, explains to us how all phenomena are created. It also shows us how these can manifest, take root and evolve in the different worlds of our universe.

The simplicity of the cosmic constitution unfortunately also shows us the depths of our ignorance. It demonstrates without comment the poverty, the intellectual feebleness of all those so-called thinkers who, from century to century, encumber our literary output, by reciting, like parrots, the same inanities in a form adapted to the mentality of the time.

These fundamental and eternal conditions of life hold sway in all the universes which exist in infinite space and demonstrate the extent of the explorations we can undertake. Original source of all the vibrations which have given birth to the many forms of living matter, the analysis of this universal substance is the first task which confronts the student.

To begin with, it is prudent to avoid the innumerable forms which roam the various planes of our universe and to concentrate on the whirling matter of these worlds.

When, by experience, we have sufficiently studied the characteristics of the most accessible planes; when we have become aware of the nature of the energies capable of manifesting these, and the conditions in which it is possible to live, then we may begin to study the forms themselves in a more rational manner.

In practice, only place a limited confidence in the shapes which manifest during your projections. You must seek to see the universal substance as a limitless atmosphere of variable density and luminosity.

The observation of the study-groups scattered about the various planes sums up the most rational experience for the average intelligence. A being who is sufficiently advanced will never waste his

time on a plane where his work has become automatic. His Higher Consciousness will quickly
bring him to a sense of reality and, with one powerful
upward urge, he will wing his way to those regions
where the main study is that of the universe and its
laws. He will experiment, will enrich his consciousness by all possible means, and in his next incarna-
tion he will be able to connect both causes and effects
with the fulfilment of the universal purpose.

It is impossible for me to give you any kind of
nomenclature for the images which are to be met in
the Invisible, as these are limitless. I repeat: No
vibration can manifest in any planet of our solar
system without its being registered on the different
planes of the cosmic atmosphere in which our
universe is evolving. Whatever may be their
appearance, their magnetic attractions, affinities,
ideas, thoughts, desires, sentiments, forces, shapes,
or wave-length, all radiations are capable of manifesting in the universal movement under the
category to which they belong.

In practice, our first efforts will be to distinguish
between thought-forms and living beings. As
examples, the following are the most common:

(1) Images created by our own thoughts.

(2) Images created by discarnate entities, dependent upon the direction of their thoughts and
affections.

(3) The ephemeral thoughts of each individual
consciousness floating at random, or towards a predetermined goal, in any grade of the universal
substance.

(4) The collective thoughts of the earth's
inhabitants.

(5) Images relative to past events, great or small.

(6) The animated double of everything which exists here below, whether of so-called inanimate objects or of living things.

(7) Living entities already well stabilized, such as plants and animals which are awaiting their earthly manifestation.

(8) The empty, worn-out shells of living beings passing from one dimension to a higher one.

(9) Human beings themselves, among which we must distinguish between those living in permanent and those in temporary forms.

Lastly, you must realize that a will greater than your own can manifest in any form, and then you may gauge the difficulties attendant upon these studies.

So far as the shapes of Higher Beings are concerned, they have none. They are autonomous centres of energy. It is easy for them to show themselves in whatever shape they wish, but, in practice, one sees them rarely. We feel their presence only by a special atmosphere which is marked by a friendly energy, full of confidence and conveying a benevolent and protective magnetism. In certain cases they express their friendship by symbols and with the sole aim of helping you.

The study of thought-forms calls for some amount of practice. The following is a procedure which I can recommend. When you understand sufficiently the first few degrees that are within your reach, then examine the world where you may happen to be by placing yourself in a substance which is slightly less material. In this way you will be able to observe at leisure all the different details without any risk of

causing any disturbance by your personal thoughts.
What is more, we are far freer in our actions as we
are in no way incommoded by the magnetism of the
world which we are studying.

Please note that this statement applies to all cases.
Study scientific phenomena from a higher dimension
and you will have the key to their explanation.

One day I was studying the constitution of earthly
objects in this way. I could see trees and plants as
if under an X-ray. I could see the fibres in a
darker tone like a vast nervous system and I could
see the sap moving along in them. In the same way
I could see the skeletons of human beings and was
surprised to note the numerous malformations of the
spine and thorax.

We appreciate the utility of a shape, or the
degree of evolution attained by a living being, by the
quality of his magnetic radiations, by the reactions
he causes in our aura, as we shall see further on in
this work.

The images of past events are easily distinguishable from those organizations whose aim is to give
instructions to the newly dead, by an activity whose
reality is beyond any power of expression.

I remember once having touched a metal shaving
thrown off by a lathe in a factory and to have
received a sensation of burning. This happened,
of course, in the state of consciousness connected
with the plane.

It is impossible to imagine the reality of this
existence and all the facts connected with it. We
ourselves placed in the same state of consciousness
as the dwellers on any given plane, feel the usefulness
of this organization, beyond the range of argument,

and would never dream of acting on these forms for the sake of mere curiosity. Just in the same way as no sane person on earth would think of breaking window-panes in order to amuse himself. The observer who is conscious of the possibilities of the higher worlds, judges this invisible life just as a university graduate would appreciate the work of a child learning to fashion a walking-stick. The usefulness is impressed upon us by the fact that we have ourselves lived through the same needs. Furthermore, it is impossible to give anyone the consciousness of a higher state if he has not become aware of the need for such in the cosmic scheme.

When it is a matter of forms representing past events the will acts more positively. All that is necessary is to will in order to make them disappear at once, just like a photograph in which we are no longer interested.

The shapes of lesser importance created in a haphazard way, without any definite consistency, dissolve fairly easily under the influence of will. We must never be too trustful of appearances. If they belong to groups it may be that we are not so strong as the people who have created them and may be ill-used by them. It is better not to take any notice of such forces.

Under the influence of thought certain shapes dissolve and leave not a trace, just like alcohol does when allowed to evaporate in the air. Others have far more resistance, and we are obliged to have a kind of struggle with them before they will go. In certain cases I noticed that a liquid residue was left behind, a thick, blackish kind of amorphous protoplasm. Sometimes it was a residue symbolic of broken glass.

After a few experiments it is easy to distinguish between thought-forms and living beings who are already developed. In the majority of cases thought-forms are less vibrant, less active than beings in evolution. Their magnetism is far less powerful. During these studies I one day had occasion to dissolve the astral form of a dog. Only the head remained, and I saw a child come towards me and tell me that it was really a dog. The intense nature of the life which animated this head made me understand my mistake at once.

When we dissolve a thought-form, the first thing we notice is a slowing down in the whirling movement of its atoms. The shape loses definition and seems to go out of focus. The dimensions change, the image grows smaller and loses cohesion, and finally disappears.

PART TWO

SOME RELATIONSHIPS BETWEEN MAN AND THE UNIVERSE

CHAPTER I

THE POWERS OF THOUGHT

ALL the processes used for communicating with the Invisible Life, of which self-projection is the crowning feat, depend on the true balance of the forms of energy which are in action in our universe, and the general scheme of which I have outlined in the previous part of this work.

Our usual conceptions enter on a new path. Morality itself leaves the premises of "right" and "duty," created by man.

The results of my experiments have shown me that human consciousness must be conjoined with a centralizing and directing system of energy beyond, though including, the temporary personality in use by the consciousness in its physical manifestation.

The key to the development of the higher faculties lies in man seeking to live and to manifest his will in harmony with the laws of nature and the system of eternal harmonies which he is about to create between himself and the universe.

The means of communication with the Invisible are fairly numerous. They vary from the most elementary spiritualistic experiment to communion of the consciousness with the higher worlds.

Thought is the tool which is used in all cases. The study of thought is of deep interest, and a knowledge of its mechanism is the elementary, indispensable basis of all psychical study.

It is sad that this mechanism is so misunderstood. The effects of thought are as positive as a material object, and its importance grows with the development of the consciousness.

Thought is the fruit of a long series of successive evolutions. It is only after innumerable attempts, extending over immense periods of time, that nature managed to endow the human being with so perfect a power.

If we push the analysis of thought down to its fundamental roots we realize that it is not a thing in itself. The act of thinking is the result of a system of energies which allow us to use images, called ideas, in order to discover either the root cause or the key to phenomena and to adapt these to our needs.

The effect of thought on ideas might well be compared to a system of metal refining. Thought compresses, moulds, and forges ideas, under the repeated assaults of the imagination, in order to make them more supple under the hammer of reason.

Under the influence of thought a whole series of unconscious processes come into play. Attention, comparison and judgment bring about a new order aimed at a goal which may be sentimental, instinctive or definitely marked out by reason.

Thought is the expression of a double relationship: "Relative" in phenomenal time; "Absolute," that is to say constant, or invariable, outside the field of attraction of our universe.

Thanks to this double relationship, consciousness can become aware of effects, deduce their causes, and extract the basic principles all by comparing them with its own nature.

To trace out these relationships would take us too far. Suffice it to say that the relationship which is variable and relative follows the different phases of experience, while the invariable relationship extracts that part which is of general usefulness, by means of which it enriches the higher consciousness.

It should be remembered that every time one thinks, an energy, roughly comparable to electricity, is brought into play. This is of a positive nature every time it extracts from the images a judgment of a generally useful character. Its action is the more intense the more it approaches an organization having for aim the common good.

The negative aspect of thought is accentuated every time it descends to ideas of disorder, disorganization, egotism, and all images such as are connected with the lower, animal instincts. In fact, it finds itself compressed by the nature of the universal substance, and this rapid breaking down gives it only an ephemeral life.

My experiments have shown me that: "thoughts of a similar nature attract each other, and thoughts of a contrary nature repel one another." Here is the origin of all association of ideas, personal or collective.

The act of returning good for evil is only the strict application of this fundamental law. In putting into practice the maxim, "an eye for an eye, a tooth for a tooth," you are increasing a system of energy which hits the weakest, let it be a hundred times in the right.   In sending thoughts of affection towards a person who wishes you ill, you raise an impenetrable wall, against which all adverse thoughts will break themselves.   If your enemy persists, a line of least resistance will be created, along which his thoughts will return to him, like a ball rebounding from a wall.

The same law can be applied, advantageously, to physical, moral or intellectual ailments, as also to the events of life.   There is nothing mysterious about this, which merely expresses elementary psychic laws.

Thought is also connected with a system of energy, used by many people, under a superstitious form.   I mean invocation or prayer.

I know from experience that it is possible to bring into play, in the Invisible, forces whose potency is proportionate to the centrifugal power of one's thoughts.   In order to live consciously in this rarefied atmosphere and have access to its reservoir of energy, it is necessary to be free from all contrary attractions.   This decentralization calls for a series of sustained efforts, up to the point where personal interest has been replaced by general interest.   We must learn to love the "constants" of this general interest in the same way that we have been used to loving ourselves.

Though this goal may seem to be far off, it is within the reach of all.   Each one of us can make the necessary efforts which, in time, will allow him to become a higher being and live in the sublime regions of space.

This ingenious mechanism of the cosmic system

being taken for granted, we may deduce from this that life is eternal, by its automatic renewal in one form or other. It is therefore not only possible, but practically certain, that a mass of human beings have already made the efforts to live constantly in the higher regions of the ether.

This semi-certainty becomes definite by experience, when we learn, in fact, of the existence of supermen, whom our ancestors used to consider as gods. The extraordinary power of their auras, the perfection of the qualities one recognizes in them, the perfect mechanism of the dimension where they are to be found, surpass in simplicity all that men could have imagined concerning the gods with which they peopled space.

When we consider their ignorance of evolutionary laws, we cannot wonder that the people of ancient times tried to find favour in the eyes of their divinities by more or less barbaric deeds. Even to-day these superstitions are carefully nursed by sects whose self-interest it is easy to understand. So we behold powerful cultural associations brandishing, according to need, either the nightmare of infernal visions or the beatitude of life in paradise.

Since access to the higher worlds is the effect of our own decentralization, and it is enough to learn to love a higher and more perfect order of things, the dogmas enunciated by religious trade unions break down lamentably.

If we follow a course of conduct which is honourable, always trying to develop a state of affairs which is more tolerant, more friendly, more brotherly, we attract towards us the notice of those high Individualities living in the superior worlds, and will thus receive help according to the loftiness of our aims.

It is, therefore, useless to invoke any saint to do our work for us. All the wealth of the world will not give access to these higher worlds into which the poorest may enter. The coin we are using is within the reach of all: It is the universal attraction directed by thought in the positive way of the universe.

Whilst, on the side of matter, energy is dispersed in a multiplicity of effects, of phenomena into which every fraction of life is imprisoned, on the side of force it is a unification of causes into a principle of activity which is one and the same Life, Thought, and Wisdom.

To direct our thoughts and desires towards the material aspect of existence, is to compress ourselves into the multiple forms of the passive state.

To take as goal the idealistic side of life, and make it part and parcel of the practical necessities of existence, is to attract towards us the positive "constants" of the universe and to become able to live in this state in absolute freedom.

When your thoughts radiate into space, remember that they become subservient to the law of Cause and Effect, like all the other forms of energy. When you are concentrating your ideas on the goal to be attained, by asking politely, under the guise of an invocation or prayer, that you should be helped in your efforts, take care to follow psychical laws. Use only such expressions as are *positive*, full of confidence and love and certainty. Avoid all ideas relative to evil, to hate, to fear, to uncertainty, to

THE POWERS OF THOUGHT

pain, to passivity, to ignorance, etc.   Only such
conceptions as are contrary to these will give you
access to the higher worlds of energy.   It is evident
that if you attract it under this form, the other tendencies of the mind will be automatically destroyed.

CHAPTER II

ILLUSION AND REALITY

WHILST reading of these relationships which, in themselves, are not so extraordinary, the reader who is not well versed in psychic matters may wonder how, during these studies, it is possible to differentiate between illusion and reality.

If you will consider the results of the experiments I have described, you will understand that the cosmic system automatically selects all forms of energy, according to their rhythms and harmonies, and distributes them either towards the crude matter or pure energy of the universe.

In these immense fields of electro-magnetic matter there are no privileges. Whatever the degree of evolution, each individual receives according to his efforts. Whether this energy contributes to his happiness or sorrow does not concern the law of Cause and Effect. The mechanism is the same in both cases.

Let us, for one moment, consider the general characteristics of the universe. In a limited space we are given a radio-active matter endowed with a potential varying from $+\cdot 1$ to $-\cdot 1$. Of itself this substance has no other function than to absorb avidly all forms of energy which present themselves

This we might call the feminine element, amenable to all influences.

An active element, movement, animates this substance. On one side a maximum of intensity and a minimum electro-motive energy balances the attractions. This is the aspect of matter, negative, ruled by centripetal force. On the other side a minimum of intensity under the influence of a maximum of voltage. This is the energy aspect, positive, ruled by centrifugal force.

Life, a neutral element, formed by a conjunction between the opposed relationships of universal movement, lies latent in all motions of the universal substance. It can manifest from a state of extreme density to the most volatile essence of our universe. It circulates freely in all forms of movement without becoming subject to any one form.

The stabilization of these low and high frequency currents creates balanced states in the universe, planes which do not intermingle. Life alone, formed by a balance of extreme elements, may penetrate within them all. In order to change from one plane to another it becomes necessary to acquire life.

This life is at the mercy of all disturbing elements, of all lack of balance occurring in any of the modes of movement in the universal substance. If an infinity is established between elements of different potential an electrical coupling will arise, the rhythm of which will evoke relationships of equal wave-length. This is the story of the mineral kingdom, visible reflection of the invisible agglomerations which exist in the universal substance.

The forms of energy circulating in the physical

matter will establish between the elements of the mineral kingdom paths of least resistance which will, in turn, bring about new affinities. These, in their turn, will take on life in the invisible worlds in order to manifest on earth at the first opportunity.

The successive addition of the resulting potentialities determinates the visible repetition of the instantaneous movement which may be observed in the formation of the intimate principles of the mineral kingdom. Instead of being born and dying almost instantaneously, the mineral elements succeed in coming together and giving each other mutual support. The result is an alternating movement, at great speed, of the life and death of the atoms; but the sum total persists, grows and finally develops into the vegetable kingdom.

The vegetable life will develop and strengthen the type of movement begun in the mineral kingdom. Observed in its own dimension, each plant already constitutes a little universe of specialized life, and soon the protozoons will appear, the rudiments of the animal kingdom.

First of all without a nucleus, then a simple unicellular organism, then association of cells, this evolution pursues its way from the simple to the complex. In the ether the movement is accentuated, the potential energy takes on greater activity and becomes visible on earth. The organs of movement collect first of all as radiations around a centre, then in pairs placed on either side of a median axis. The disturbing affinity, manifested by a specialized form of life, has been considerably transformed. Endowed with a certain sensitivity it seeks out similar elements and grows by means of all the affinities it can capture. It attaches itself to these, clings on, and thereby increases its power and its capacity for life.

This elementary mechanism of life, visible and invisible, opens out fresh horizons on all the phenomena of evolution.

Since there are constant relationships between the same potential of life, whether visible or invisible, the evolution of the system of harmonies which it represents falls into normal conditions. Whether this vital potential be called mineral, vegetable, animal, or human, it is the same principle which is perfecting itself, ever drawn towards the positive aspect of its own system in the universe.

We know, by experience, that this primitive aspect represents a maximum of forces, of electromagnetic power, with a minimum of density. The rarefication of this force is such that freedom is almost absolute, and the manipulation of this energy determines the greatest number of effects with the least effort.

The observation of facts shows us all the affinities directing themselves towards the positive side of the universe. Life follows these groupings, whose autonomy becomes more defined as they perfect themselves.

Affinity, desire, sentiment, are all so many disturbing causes which are capable of taking on life in the universal substance. It is therefore natural that the human being should be attracted constantly by these elementary lives. To these man represents the centre of the universe. From this results an attraction on the part of man towards the material side of life, towards ephemeral pleasure of all kinds, and this attraction of living matter is one of the normal facts of evolution.

Writers who can only conceive of egotism as the basis of our activities are only obeying this law of nature. But, if they favour the evolution of the universal substance in the lower kingdoms they are delaying their personal evolutionary processes.

The way of life, on our particular planet, seems therefore to teach us that personal disinterestedness is a form of spiritual egotism. This would be true if the Love of Unity did not intervene. This sends back into multiplicity the benefit which has been acquired by personal evolution.

The mechanical detachment from the lower forms of life, with the sole aim of perfecting ourselves and living in the higher regions of the universe, would certainly give results. The human being could be generous, altruistic on principle, all the time retaining at the core of his being a feeling of individuality to which he would bring back the fruit of his labours.

I find this quite in accordance with reality, and there are many philosophers who have never been able to find a higher ideal.

The experience of self-projection in the higher regions of the cosmos confirms us in the possibility of desiccation of consciousness. However great the degree of evolution reached by an initiate working in self-interests, he will never be able to escape from the universal system in which he is born, because the marriage between the higher consciousness and cosmic consciousness calls for the abandonment of all the personal element. Having entered into the circle of manifested life in our system through egotism, the consciousness which results can only leave by abandoning the root of personality. Its freedom is then limitless, because it is working in harmony with the Universal Order, procreator of all the finite systems floating in infinite space.

This, therefore, is the definite result to which we come when we wish to differentiate between what is real and what is illusionary in our universe. All words, all forms of expression, seem to have been invented by the human being in order to hide his ignorance of the universal life.

Reality is one word, illusion is another. Both are necessities of evolution. What is real on earth is illusion in the next plane, and so on. But without earthly illusion there would be no higher reality. Each living element possesses its portion of both illusion and reality, one being as necessary as the other, since they transform themselves reciprocally.

CHAPTER III

EVOLUTION IN TIME AND SPACE

THE absolute, experimental reality of the worlds existing within the various densities of the cosmic ether, gives a new sense of value to our scientific knowledge.

The idea of energy appears, through all its innumerable transformations, like a universal Proteus. The atom, of electric nature, creates in its seething whirlpools an extraordinary suppleness of matter, and gives the man who is living in that matter powers and faculties which are semi-divine.

During experience it appears as if these fields of ether and electro-magnetic super-ethers had simpler and simpler dimensions which, successively, penetrate to the most dense matter. It is quite easy to realize that the converse does not exist. In finding their proper position, the delicacy and sensibility of the vibrations respond to a scale of powers more extended in time and space.

We could visualize this atmosphere as a series of waves sustaining themselves by resonance. It is natural that the human will can create the phenomena of interference by an exchange of potentialities drawn from its surroundings.

However far we pursue our researches, observation shows us that life animates a matter which is pure energy capable of responding to weaker and weaker stimuli the further it radiates into a greater space with, naturally, atoms which are far less densely packed together. It seems as if the limit of centrifugal exteriorization is lost in infinite space.

Our system of universes seems, then, to be a gathering of finite worlds, radiating into the infinite by quantum, and the extreme limit of this radiation is the point of contact with infinity.

For the person who can push his experiments into these sublimated regions of the universe, the progressive subtlety of the succeeding states of matter, the increase in powers, the unity of the faculties which have the capacity for instantaneous self-realization in absolute freedom permits him to approach the constitution of the universe with a total of probability hitherto unknown.

We are in the presence of:

(1) A matter in constant motion, progressively obedient to our needs, in a manner which becomes speedier and more intense.

(2) An intelligence conscious both of the unity and universality of its powers, which it can put into action in either a fraction or the whole of the spherical space which it occupies, in a measure exactly proportionate to its power. It is capable of rest or movement with no interval of time occurring between the two states.

This extreme mobility, beyond all conceptions of time and space, gives us some indication that the human being has succeeded in creating, for his personal use, a system of harmonies allowing him to control his own movements, without having recourse to the limited forms of energy.

Energy is limited by two factors—time and space. Comparison and deduction from facts warrant the conclusion that the evolution of the living atom has in view the conquest of these two elements so necessary to our universe.

Time, destroyer of all forms of energy, is the first agent against which the battle rages. All living atoms collect together in order to fight it. They cling tenaciously to everything favourable to their existence and no individuality would ever have seen daylight without egotism or this centralization of atoms.

After numberless peregrinations throughout the kingdoms of nature, the living being begins to develop an energy system endowed with resonances sufficiently powerful to allow it to endure.

The analysis of the different states of consciousness in the various regions of space permits me to conclude that the human being denoted a definite stage in the universal struggle against time which was being waged by individualized life.

Space being conditioned by time, a great victory has been won. The materials accumulated by the living being in the different kingdoms of nature have balanced themselves to produce a higher form of energy, and now the animal has been transformed into a human being.

The uninitiated, never having become aware of the modalities of force in the universal substance, cannot imagine the formidable amount of energy which corresponds to this new title. And, without exaggeration, we may conclude that the human being is immortal in "Time." Please take note that I carefully specify "in Time."

This is a matter of extreme importance to our evolution. In fact, the human being, representing the triumph of life over time, has no more cause to worry. This struggle for existence constituted the first stage of his independence. It was necessary for a maximum of energy to be collected in order that his vital potential might find sufficient nourishment, whilst recover its forces so soon as they were exhausted, without being limited by the duration of the process.

We may consider the vital potential of the living being as a system of waves which tend to weaken and disintegrate under the influence of time. The centripetal action of energy balances this destructive influence. The living being profits from this provisional help of nature in order to amass the materials necessary to the preservation of life. The struggle against time soon takes on a new character. As it develops, the animal's system of whirling atoms allows it to become aware of the higher forms of life. These elements of consciousness will become more perfect, up to the moment when a final impulse will balance them with a neutral state in the Cosmos placed half-way in the total evolution of the universe.

In order to make our ideas more definite, let us suppose that in this state there is, for example, 50 per cent of matter and 50 per cent of force, then the centripetal and centrifugal actions are in equilibrium. In this density matter possesses an intermediatery unity between the extremity of dense matter and the extremity of pure energy. The balance is perfect from the point of view both of matter and energy. The living being who has succeeded in reaching this state possesses therefore at this moment a system of atoms capable of maintaining its own movement without recourse to centripetal energy. Internal pressure balances external pressure. The weakening and subsequent destruction of the efforts exerted need not be feared. Life is no longer limited by time. This is the birth of human consciousness.

Granted the experimental nature of the universe, each one of us can appreciate the efforts necessary to realize this new consciousness. At the moment it is obvious that the human consciousness is ignorant of its possibilities. By analogy we may compare it to the birth of the living being. The first whirlpools of cosmic substance, which have acquired life, are going to use this life in order to increase their personal energy, and little by little reach this intermediary cosmic state, where a new birth awaits them. This awakening is for the animal a kind of illumination. Without understanding its characteristics it becomes aware of being a unity. It feels as One in the midst of the surrounding energy. It has now become an individuality.

If you have understood the extremely simple mechanism of the universe you should be able to see at once this second part of evolution, which concerns us all. The living being, now become a conscious unity, is going to work in order to conquer the space which separates him from the other extremity of the Cosmos. Up to the present the centripetal energy preponderated. Now it is the centrifugal force which is going to allow the energy of the human being to radiate, and this extension will go on progressively until the extremity of pure force in matter is reached. The balance which, up to then, was internal and centralized, will now transform itself into an external balance, circumferential. This is easy to understand. To the centrifugal states, to the planes, dimensions and densities of the second part of the cosmos correspond the centripetal states, planes, densities, and dimensions of the first part of evolution. In radiating an external energy the human being helps the growth of the previous states in which he has already lived as an animal entity. In proportion to his advance towards the aspect of force, so do his radiations fall towards matter, the characteristics of which he now learns to discern. This awareness of the past gives the human consciousness an understanding of the causes and principles which will become its only food, allowing it to live in the atmosphere of the higher worlds. As it becomes able to obtain nourishment in a more rarefied substance the consciousness soon reaches the extremity of pure energy. Consciousness has now vanquished space. The new equilibrium which is the result of this feat gives it a neutral nature similar to the life whose characteristics it takes on. The consciousness, as a unity, becomes a multiplicity and free of the Cosmic Universe in which it was born.

In this evolutionary scheme one fact of great importance should be kept in mind, i.e. that the human entity has no further interest in remaining egotistical. On the contrary, egotism and self-centredness hinder him from becoming aware of, and realizing, the causes and principles which are going to become his only nourishment in the higher worlds. Egotism will hold him back to lower planes. It hinders the radiation of energy towards the matter side. It becomes a terrible obstacle to the casting away of ties, a process indispensable to the evolution of the human being towards freedom, towards the pure energy aspect of the universal substance. The human being has no longer any need to be egotistical as he has become independent of the time factor. He is no longer in the same cycle. In order to conquer time, he has had to accumulate around him the greatest possible amount of energy. In order to become master of space the human being must decentralize himself by returning to nature the energy which he has borrowed. Time, the great destroyer, seeks in some way to tear up, to dissociate, the forms built up by energy. The living being attracts to himself, centralizes, closes in, and, aided by centripetal force, holds time in check by a constant attraction which is, egotistically, centred on his personality. When he acquires equilibrium he becomes free.

Having passed through all forms of life, the human being proceeds to examine these manifestations, with the help of the new faculties which will be developed by the use of thought. In becoming aware of the causes of phenomena he also becomes free of the forms of the universal substance. These interest him all the less because he realizes that he is able to reproduce them at will, simply by putting into practice the causes which rule them.

By centring his affections on principles which embrace a whole number of phenomena the human entity, little by little, escapes from the general movement which holds in equilibrium the atoms of our

system of worlds.   He frees himself progressively
from the attractions which force him to gravitate to
the "interior" of this system of energies.   His personal formation draws nearer to the speed of the
universe in which he lives.   Soon he arrives at the
point of contact between his planetary system and
the infinite.   By decentralizing himself he has conquered space and is no longer the slave of the
obligations which limit the living beings in the
universe from which he has just escaped.

CHAPTER IV

SOME LIGHT ON THE FORMATION OF THE UNIVERSE

AFTER the preceding chapters, we can try to work up to the probable causes upon which are based the existence of our universe.

The clairvoyant mind will be able to build up the skeleton of a system of forces by remembering the fundamental principles of its experiences. In the universal movement any disturbance of equilibrium of energy is readjusted by a balance of forces under another aspect. The result of this is that no atom is ever taken away nor is one ever added; there is only a transformation of energy from one state to another.

In practice we must remember that when one form of energy rises, another of equal value falls; and when a conjunction of two atoms is achieved a double expansion surges from the point of balance. The evolution of this point continues, therefore, in an inverse manner; and mobile forces change their direction in accordance with the new cycle. We shall see this interesting idea again in greater detail later on, as being the basis of all cosmic formations.

For the moment I only want to give you some of the results of special experiments which place the problem of the creation of worlds and universes on new ground.

I have already written of that fundamental experience, probably the most important, and at any rate one of the most clear and conscious that I have ever obtained in the higher worlds. I am writing of that synthetic consciousness which I have called Unity-Multiplicity, in which I managed, for a single instant, to place myself in the full knowledge and understanding of Cause as such.

In this condition man is a god. In the orbit of his Love, his life is at once everywhere and nowhere. The space in which this formless, divine energy radiates, is impregnated with his life. Not an atom can be influenced, not a single vibration can be produced, without his being immediately aware of it. This Unity-Multiplicity energy of the higher worlds makes it difficult even to remember the feeble powers of the earthly state. No comparison is possible between the two. I cannot repeat too often the fact that we feel quite as much a whole in each part as we do in the sum total. Whether we act everywhere at once or at some given point in spherical space, it is by means of an impulse which comes from the entire being.

Human consciousness has been transformed into an energy which is stable, serene, and immutable, endowed with an immense power of attraction, capable of producing movement in a considerable space without the intrinsic energy of this consciousness having been either augmented or diminished by one iota.

Omniscience, omnipotence, omnipresence, are all summed up in one universal Consciousness of Life and Love. All powers are held in a single universal capacity for awakening and developing latent energy within the depths of the eternal silence of limitless space.

Let us now consider some of the characteristics of the virgin substance which lies outside and beyond our evolutionary system. On several occasions I was brought into the presence of an atmosphere which had none of the usual properties of the substance of our universe.

This new substance had the property of a kind of mechanical inertia. In the successive ethers of the universe the matter of any one given stratum responds with an intensity which varies with our personal vibrations. Thousands of ties make us aware of the fact that we are in touch, through our own system of atoms, with the surrounding universe, and experience shows that the link becomes more intimate in the higher worlds.

The virgin matter into which I projected myself exhibited no ties like those mentioned above. Neither thought, desire, will, nor any attraction of our own world has power over this matter, and equally, the matter has no magnetic effect on us.

Seen in bulk, this matter has the colour of freshly cut ebonite. It gives out no vibration. It has no elasticity. Whereas in our system the radio-active emanations of matter increase the joy of living and feeling, here we feel nothing, and we are not aware of the very least reaction. According to the density of this virgin substance so we have the impression of standing before a thick wall or in a mist, neither so solid nor so dark. Whichever may be the case, in order to penetrate into it we must make a definite mechanical effort. With arms outstretched we must push this matter aside in order to break through, when we have the quite material sensation of moving in a sort of "paste" which does not stick and is not cloying. In an atmosphere which is not so dense, all that we need do is to make the motion of wrapping it around us, just as we would put on a cloak.

This substance without cohesion has always puzzled me. When we are projected into this kind of atmosphere we feel that we are thrown upon our own resources. Though the powers of thinking, reasoning, and consciousness itself are clear, they have not the sensitivity even of that experienced in the lowest strata of our cosmic ether.

Deeply immersed in this gluey matter, which I was handling as if it were some material object, I compared its characteristics, which are so different from those of our own system; and I placed in opposition to it, by the power of thought, the vibrant sweetness and delicacy of the extra-sensitive waves of astral matter.

The existence of a substance so material led me to suppose that it might well be the root of matter.

Let us admit for a moment that this stagnant, motionless, vibrationless matter, this ebonite-coloured atmosphere, this veil of substance without ties of any kind, is the virgin state of the matter existing without form in the infinite.

Let us place it in the presence of the prerogatives of the Unity-Multiplicity consciousness. Then tell me who amongst you would not be eager to bring these two results of experimentation together?

With the extraordinary faculties which have been acquired by evolution, where is the superman who would not do his best to make this matter more supple, to mould it, to try, by all the means known to him, to transmit some of his own energy into it so as to make it responsive to a "stimulus"?

To sum up, are we not here face to face with the very principle by which the universe was formed? This very principle would urge the consciousness to make this matter sufficiently supple to transform a mechanical energy into a field of electro-magnetic energy, for instance, to make life spring forth by creating an equilibrium of the forces brought into action. Life could then make use of this matter by means of the affinities which would be present. Lastly, we would extract these from the full consciousness of manifestations and their phenomenal causes.

For the moment I do not propose labouring further the point which concerns the mystery of our origin. My aim was to point out these two opposite principles. One of them is endowed with conscious life, with universal powers, outside time and space. The other with latent energy, limitless, sleeping in the womb of Eternity. Let it once happen that the former acts on the latter and a whole new system of energies will be born, following upon this first wave of universalized life.

In our system of worlds, everything happens as if the order of its reigning forces were obedient to a plan, to a scheme of action which knows of no exceptions.

This scheme, this evolutionary plan seems itself

to be tied to other plans of evolution which have already come to an end, and having as goal the preparation of the elements of new worlds which will also be only one of the multiple aspects of the universal order.

CHAPTER V

THE FUNDAMENTAL PRINCIPLE OF HUMAN LIFE

THE information which I have been able to draw from the invisible side of our system of worlds has to some extent allowed me to make a valuation of the fundamental factors of existence.

The increased subtility, under the influence of the universal matter-force which exists in the various grades of the ether, allows the human being a far greater range of powers with far lesser expenditure of energy, and more instantaneous results.

The human being's personal evolution, that is to say his successive mouldings in the universal matter, has, as its aim, the facilitating of this apprenticeship.

Attraction is the universal form of energy in the worlds of the cosmos reduced to its simplest expression.

If we consider the question in terms of infinity, attraction can have no meaning. The fact that an atom may be drawn towards the centre or the circumference of a magnetic field does not change its absolute value in the least.

In a system whose dimensions are limited, attraction takes on a value which is relative to the factors which have to be taken into consideration. It is easy to realize the fact that attraction, viewed from a central point of radiation, will be called repulsion if it directs itself towards the periphery, and vice versa. The word repulsion is relative to the position of the observer.

In order to differentiate itself from the mass, a coupling of energy is forced to resist the dual current of equilibrium and unbalancement which has been produced by one point displacing itself in order to travel towards another. To this end it will centralize and focus itself, and will assimilate all the atoms of energy of an equal rhythm and periodicity. Thus we realize that what we know as a human being is nothing more than a system of energies which has been successful in assimilating a range of harmonic vibrations which are sufficient for it to maintain its balance in time.

If you reflect on what I have already written you will realize that time represents the action of the centrifugal force on the matter side of the universal substance. By progressively resisting this action the human being manages to nourish himself in a type of matter where the two forces, centripetal and centrifugal, produce a balance in an equal proportion of both crude matter and pure energy. We can claim that the time factor has been conquered. The space factor, which the human being is going to learn to master, is nothing more than the action of the centripetal force, which stretches from this point of equilibrium to the extreme limit of pure energy in the universal substance.

Time and space are no more than the aspects of universal attraction functioning in its two modes, centrifugal and centripetal.

In pure reality infinite space is represented by the

tiniest possible material atom and infinite time by the most powerful form of energy. These two balance each other. The expressions, time and space, are therefore not able to define the state in which the human consciousness finds itself in the uttermost depths of eternity. The time-space in which it finds itself, is, in reality, nothing more than a point of the universal movement in equilibrium. It is a point of attraction without dimension, the exterior pressure of which balances the interior pressure, and which has neither size nor duration.

Since attraction is the fundamental pivot, the eternal pulse of the Formless Energy vibrating in the womb of the eternal present, it is natural that the observations made on the confines of our world of being should confirm this principle.

After having registered all the attractions of the system in which he is evolving, the living entity, who has now become the human being, must rid himself of all form in order to keep one thing only—the personal equation.

To remain in a condition of stasis, without desire, without thought, without affection of any kind, is a poor solution to the problem.

Experience demonstrates that it is necessary to unify these desires, thoughts, and affections all towards the same point, directing them by love towards a more perfected state of things.

Whatever the state of development of an individual, this principle applies to all.

The energy to use is conscious thought, coupled with an ever-growing affection for all manifestations of the Good, the Beautiful, and the True. These manifestations become unified, little by little, into strata of consciousness which are less differentiated. They lose their material support and resolve themselves into a conscious unity, first-fruit of universal Love.

If we consider the really practical aspect of human existence, if we decide, once and for all, to bring out the very principle of his existence, to discover the intrinsic energy by which he is animated, it is in this general attraction of the fundamental principles of the world that we must delve.

Speaking for myself, having been able to appreciate the wonderful perfection of the scheme of things in the state of Unity-Multiplicity, all this is an indisputable certainty. The fusing of the universal and the particular gives human consciousness the most perfect of prerogatives imaginable.

The idea of a divinity ruling heaven and earth is easily understood. In imagining the possibilities of their gods, human beings were simply experiencing an intuition concerning their personal destiny.

Whatever may be the opinions and beliefs of any individual, experience permits me to affirm, without a shadow of doubt, the absolute reality of a universal principle of attraction, fundamental in nature, which unites human beings the one with the other and with the universe.

In order that the human being may become a centre of independent life, free from all cosmic formations, and may participate consciously in the full realization of the laws of the universe, he must be placed in agreement with the harmonies of which they are constituted.

As the harmonies of the universal order act at one and the same time on the past and the future, in a present which is outside the scope of our measuring ability, it is useless to encumber ourselves with definitions. Far better for each of us to assimilate, little by little, states of consciousness which are more extended, more profound, and to put into action the principle of attraction which lies within every living being.

Under different names this principle exercises its activity within all and every degree of evolution. Whether it be in the guise of affinity, instinct, desire, sentiment, ideal, it allows the consciousness a means of maintaining itself in a more abstract manner. The better to conceive this abstraction, instead of regarding space as extending towards the horizon, visualize it concentrating towards you. This space, coming as it does from infinity, has no limits. According to the intensity with which you condense your energy more and more to a point, so do you increase the relationship between the infinitely great and the infinitely small, and this is enough to gain access to the directing principles of the world.

In freeing yourself from all the forms with which your mentality is encumbered, by concentrating all your motives for action on to one point of view, you reduce the space you are occupying to its most simple expression.

This condensation frees you from that part of the universal substance which we know as crude matter. It allows you to centre your conscious faculties on a point of pure energy outside the reach of the cosmic currents. It leads you, with absolute inevitability, to the eternal present outside the limitations of time and space, and to a consciousness of the Universal

Order. This absolute certainty which may be acquired by practical experience of self-projection into the various densities of the universal substance, is a mechanical necessity of the universe to which everyone must submit. It is impossible to change from one state or dimension to another without leaving behind the heavier atoms of the matter in which we may find ourselves.

Whilst we are living on this earth, we can become acquainted with the other worlds only by means of a provisional projection, or by definite physical death which gives you a full freedom of action. The law is the same for all the realms of the invisible. We can only reach a higher state by casting off heavier atoms. To rid oneself of encumbering atoms means that we must leave behind our present affections in order to replace them by others of a higher nature. From which we may conclude the existence of two evolutionary principles which are mutually complementary. The first consists of mastering our lower nature. The second demands progressive centration of consciousness in a more elevated class of sentiments.

In order to put this mechanical necessity on the part of the universe into words which are within the grasp of any mentality, I would say that each one must try ceaselessly to discern an order of things superior to that in which he habitually exists. Better still, we should seek to free ourselves from our usual affections in order that we may be able to replace them by emotions of a higher order. This goes on *ad infinitum*. As soon as our motives for action have changed in value we must envisage still higher ones.

The practice of the higher love brings results which cannot be compared with the effort necessary for its exercise. In this evolutionary process there are no privileged people. Whatever one's social position, the law is at the disposal of everyone. All that has to be done is to love a little more each day.

To love nature for the sake of what it brings forth, for its beauty, for its harmony, will help to bring you a little nearer to perfection.

To feel love for the life in the mechanism which I have just described, to love that supreme justice which gives to each one in proportion to his attachment to the laws of harmony which are part and parcel of the universal order, will raise you effortlessly towards the higher worlds.

To feel love for humanity in the sweetness of spiritual communion, in the joy of helping one another, in the happiness of playing a part together in the everlasting work of the formation of worlds and universes, will bring you all the nearer to the goal of evolution.

I would like all my readers to realize that, at this point, we are no longer working out probabilities. The sum total of human opinion cannot alter this experimental certainty by one iota. Those feeble spirits who allow themselves to be influenced by so-called scientific arguments, philosophic and religious speculations, only increase their suffering and reduce their chances of finding a permanent happiness.

Let us look back for a moment. Realize the abominable way in which you are being exploited materially, morally, and intellectually. Decide, once and for all, to conquer the routine existence and preconceptions of our social state. Believe me, you will never regret having made the effort. Instead of increasing your suffering by cursing fate, you will now create an atmosphere of peace favourable to your aims if you finally decide to love a little more each day this spiritual harmony in which and for which we live.

CHAPTER VI

THE MAIN CHARACTERISTICS OF THE ATTRACTIVE PRINCIPLES IN THE INVISIBLE WORLDS

IT has been demonstrated, by physics, that if we displace a metallic circuit in a magnetic field, we induce an electric current.

On the other hand, the passage of an electric current in a conductor determines the radiation of a magnetic field, lines of least resistance when compared with the other forms of energy moving in the atmosphere.

When studying the matter of the other worlds, the principle upon which this law is based becomes of primary importance. Not only does the displacement of a point, or of an organization of energies, produce a powerful radiation, but further, all the atoms are the seat of vibrations which depend on their own particular nature. Therefore, in reality, we find ourselves in a field of multiple influences, ruled by the law of Cause and Effect, in circumstances which are still to be determined.

At all events there is one fact of which we can be sure, i.e. that the organization of whirling atoms used by the human consciousness, as a means of transport throughout the space of our system of the universe, is a marvellous detector. Extremely sensitive to the influence of the will, it automatically selects the forms of energy to which we are accustomed. Therefore each one of us, in the invisible realms, is going to attract automatically, according to his or her affections, the elements desired.

In order to make sound experimental observations, it becomes indispensable to free ourselves from all personal affections, and centre the consciousness in the Universal Order. Only by complying with this condition is it possible to obtain much information concerning the attracting qualities of the various shapes of living beings when seen in comparison with the utter perfection of the universe.

The closer we draw to the atmosphere of the higher planes the more sensitive becomes the human consciousness. The shades of understanding with which this consciousness has now become familiar increase in value and intensity. The atmosphere seems to be impregnated with the highest and most perfect qualities. Every atom takes on a special tone in agreement with the harmony of eternity, and we can see in them a world of realization which affects the consciousness in its most intimate depths.

The following are some of the realizations to which I have come through practical experience of conscious self-projection.

In the ordinary strata which we visit, the observation of personal or collective thought-forms causes us to be definitely influenced by their radiations. The attention of the observer, who has placed himself in the conditions which I have just mentioned, is attracted in a proportionate manner to the high nature of the general character of these. The vibrations which emanate from this atmosphere make us admire, with varying intensity, the part of beauty, of exactitude of expression, the whole variety of shades which are expressed by the idea. At the same time we feel an attraction, which is variable according to the forms taken on by energy, which stimulates the experimenter, who is observing, to take part in their perfection.

When it is a question of forms having a certain degree of evolution, as in the case of minerals and plants, we are attracted towards them with an intensity which corresponds with their degree of *beauty*.

When we are dealing with the animal kingdom, the attraction doubles its intensity at a rate proportionate to the degree of *goodness*.

Between the forms which are created by personal or collective thoughts and the individualized consciousness of the mineral, vegetable, and animal kingdoms, there is one particular factor which must be kept in mind.

So far as the former are concerned, all that is given out comes from the intelligence alone. So far as the latter are concerned, it is no longer a matter of merely sending out a thought, but we feel an absolute loss of energy which leaves us with an intensity which varies according to the affection we experience. This affection, vibrant with pure joy, which links us, if only for a moment, with the living beings with whom we come into contact, is, equally, in proportion to the degree of *"goodness,"* which we feel at their approach.

One day my guides gave me a task to carry out in the dark part of the ether. I was so struck by the difference between the higher worlds and the state in which I found myself that I put down the following notes. I had long been in the habit of projecting myself, and my double had been organized to resist any pressure due to the surrounding atmosphere.

The quality of the substance in which I found myself did not provoke any disagreeable sensations. I brought my attention to bear on the work to be accomplished, and the joy I felt was due merely to attraction. The joy to which we are subject is quite different in the higher worlds. It is more delicate, more sensitive, more refined. An infinite sweetness plunges the consciousness into a variety of shades of feeling. Each of the shades has its own special qualities and the whole becomes unified in a Love, a plenitude of life surging towards the eternal principle of the Cosmic Harmony.

In the lower worlds the consciousness has no other objective but the work to be undertaken. All its concentration is centred on the accomplishment of its work in a manner as near to perfection as possible. When I underwent the above-mentioned experience I had the feeling of giving a part of my life in the effort which I was making, and from this I experienced a deep-rooted happiness and infinite joy. But this joy and happiness were quite distinct from the gentle, sublimated atmosphere of the higher planes. It was a joy which was purely attractive, vital, so to speak, without reflexes. This state is found to be quite normal to us when we arrive at the necessary stratum of space.

.   .   .   .

We will now examine the quality of the attractions which we feel, in the invisible worlds, towards human beings.

As you should know, in the invisible worlds humanity possesses a character quite different from that which we know on earth. The mask of hypocrisy which we use in our social relations no longer exists. Sexual differences are no more. Men or women, young or old, are no more than centres of life radiating different qualities of energy which they have assimilated during their successive incarnations. In the aura of these people we find the affections and desires which have guided their motives for action.

When we meet people whom we have known on earth, the dominant links between us are dependent on the kind of affections which brought us together. The power of radiation of these affections possesses an intensity in proportion to their upliftment towards the eternal principles of life.

Also, when we rise towards the higher worlds, only the most powerful affections may penetrate there. They may only find a place by casting off all egotistical vibrations.

It was in this manner that, on the occasion when I was in the wonderful state of Unity-Multiplicity, a vibration of love reached me. At that very instant I knew the nature of this vibration, and the individual from whom it came; and I acted in the direction, towards the emitting energy, with an exact intensity of reactive force. This person was living on earth. Nothing can describe the infinite sweetness with which I swept aside the egotistical ingredient of this affection, which seemed to form an obstacle to the extension of my radiation into space.

From this arises a point of importance to every-one. If you want to be united truly, eternally, with those you love, you must vibrate in harmony with them on all the planes, and in every kind of activity. The more intimate the communion of thoughts and desires, the less will be the separation. I shall not waste time over the false friendships of to-day. The feeble links of mere habit weaken rapidly and have no influence in the higher worlds.

The ladder of affection has many rungs. A few observations on this subject may well follow.

On many repeated occasions I went astrally to see an old friend, of the same regiment as myself, who died during the Great War. He told me his impressions, and I reminded him of our deep friendship, and compared his state with my own. By a form of mutual understanding I was able to make him aware of the satisfaction I experienced in being near him, consciousness simultaneously in astral and physical life. I pointed out to him this inevitable outcome of my studies, about which we had so often spoken when we were in the army together. On his part, he often asked for my help in assisting other comrades of whose death I was not aware. This I did with great happiness, being both joyful and grateful to him for his good thoughts.

The quality of such attractions is marked by a real brotherhood, made up of reciprocal frankness and help, without the least egotistical reservation. Each person remains himself, without loss of individuality, whilst giving to others everything within his strength and means. Apart from the intimate pleasure of finding one another again, a tie of spontaneous affection is mixed with this. One will explain what he has seen and ask for explanations, while the other will tell what he knows and has learned. It is a mutual exchange of sympathetic thoughts which does not go beyond the particular nature of the plane where people find themselves. This is a truth which knows of no exception. If a friend or a parent were able to become conscious of the characteristics of a higher life, this analysis would enter into another category concerning the loftier regions of the Invisible.

When we meet a parent in our astral journeys the shades of affection which we have just analysed are complicated with further feelings of recognition and devotion.

I have often visited my father, who died before I began to study the invisible life, and I have always noticed definite differences between the emotion I felt towards him and he towards me (as two people are actually aware of each other in this state), from other forms of affection.

There exists an affectionate bliss in filial love which is a gift in itself. We feel willing to give more and more in order to avoid pain. This kind of love seems to be composed of the thousands of ties formed by the memories of past lives which we have spent with our dear ones, and especially of the true feelings towards ourselves of which our parents have given ample proof.

A lesson may be drawn from the above, that of learning to love children for their own sakes. Children are not toys whose only purpose is to amuse us, and over whom we have every right.

Whatever may be the title: parent, guide, protector, or master of a human being, whether visible or invisible, his basic duty is to unite the elements of the human soul which has been placed under his, or her, care into a special form. Whether this form is composed of earthly or etheric substance, it must be such as to allow its bearer to put into action the special qualities of the plane on which that soul finds itself.

On this plane our duty is clear: To give our children a maximum of knowledge in order that they may be able to use their energies in the best conditions for obtaining results.

At the same time we should give them instruction on the true nature of the universe, so that gradually they may become free from the formal conventions of our social system and centre their affections on the indestructible principles of evolution.

This gentle work of initiation allows both parents and children to form wonderful ties, which will prepare the human souls for their future communion in the mighty harmony of the higher worlds.

CHAPTER VII

SOME EXPERIENCES CONCERNING THE FUSION OF
TWIN SOULS

As far as I have been able to gather, human consciousness is of a dual nature, feminine and masculine. It can therefore stabilize its energy outside the Time-Space system of the universe.

Apart from its evolutionary nature, the separation into sexes is due to fundamental causes about which there is no certainty.

My experimental observations have shown me that there exist special affinities between consciousnesses, one of which has feminine and the other masculine tendencies. These tendencies in the course of evolution balance themselves in one individual. It is at this point that the union between twin-souls seems to take place.

Besides this union, this human duality destined to form a tertiary system which will live in an eternal reality, another force comes into play. There seems to exist between all consciousnesses an intimate communion, whose main characteristics I should like to point out to you.

Having been in an essence subtle enough to make out the details that I am setting forth, I have observed and analysed the attraction stimulated in myself by the presence of a Friend whose acquaintanceship I made on the invisible planes. These attractions are so complex and so different from our earthly conceptions that it was some time before I could educate my consciousness to register these harmonies.

When I had managed to balance my consciousness with this new state I was able to realize some quite new facts concerning our evolution. As clearly as a material object, I noted a quadruple expression of affections, formed by a double nature of conscious fraternity, the masculine and the feminine parts of the two souls, and a double affinity, equally conscious, between the masculine part of one soul and the feminine of the other.

On one side I seemed to be protected by the tenderness of an older, loving brother, whilst, on the other side, it seemed as if I were the protector, gentle and devoted, of a soul both delicate and sensitive. At the same time I felt in my most intimate depths the infinitely gentle penetration of the feminine aspect of this soul, whilst I gave out, with happiness and bliss, the corresponding fraction of my own being into the soul of my friend, with whom this exchange was carried out. The whole seemed to synthesize into a deep and reciprocal love whose nature was steeped in an eternal state of limitless devotion.

This quadruple communion of souls is the state which awaits all human beings when they reach the end of their evolution. It is useless for me to insist on the difficulty we meet with regard to expressing such an infinite complexity of shades of feeling which, in fact, vary with each one of us. The description, the general outline can be accepted as true, but the personal element gives this spiritual communion an intensity, a brilliancy, a depth, a variety of reactions which it is impossible to express in mere words. Earthly means of expression limit our definitions of the magnificence of life in the higher worlds through lack of possible comparisons.

We might try to express these ideas by means of musical symphonies of unbelievable sweetness, and even then only obtain crude results in comparison with this living reality of the divine planes.

Apart from this communion between consciousnesses, which is one of the finest triumphs of evolution, the union between twin-souls is a fact peculiar to each one of us.

As a result of personal observation in the invisible realms it seems as if, at the beginning of manifestation, two cells, or two separate systems of whirling atoms if you prefer the phrase, had been fecundated by opposite aspects of the same Principle. Progressing separately, they will once more come together at the end of evolution in order to form a unity which will never again know separation.

This union between twin-souls expresses itself on the higher planes as a state of Unity-Multiplicity which may be described, without fear of error, in the following terms: Light and intelligence; universal love and self-surrender. So long as these principles have not reached perfection, separation exists.

I shall not insist in any way on the private nature

of the experiences I propose setting down at this stage. I count on the nobility and loyalty of my readers to understand that I am publishing these facts from a feeling of brotherhood and with only one aim, to show that I am inventing nothing, that I am not putting down any detail in this book without having had full conscious control of it, in a state of full mastery of myself, and with perfect freedom of mind. Such are the circumstances in which I was enabled to obtain the following interesting observations.

I had used my ability to travel in the fourth dimension in order to pay periodical visits to a young woman who, later on, became my wife. After we had met three or four times on the physical plane circumstances intervened to separate us one from the other by several hundreds of miles. It was then that, without knowing either the town or the house where she was living, I used to go to her every night, by means of self-projection, and it was whilst in this state that we became engaged. These projections over a great distance were of great use to me. They allowed me to make a mass of observations on the nature of time and space, on the bringing into action of our personal energy, and on the various hindrances which we are likely to meet on the way. My fiancée was able to confirm, by letter, the exactness of the details about which I wrote.

When I was near to her, my impressions would translate themselves into a deep feeling of love, composed of brotherly devotion and of a general attraction of all the molecules of my astral body.

On her side my fiancée would feel my presence

and speak to me, mentally, without being able to see me. Whatever might be the place where she happened to be, whatever she might be doing, she would immediately have the very definite feeling that I was near her, and if her attention was engaged she would ask me to come again a little later.

For the most part our meetings took place in her room. She had the sensation of finding herself near a focus of energy from which she constantly received waves of great intensity. She was able to perceive my thoughts as easily as I could receive hers. In such a situation the only difference between thought and word lies in the greater facility and speed of self-expression. The relative states of consciousness of the two beings are translated by each, with precision and without ambiguity. It was with a sweetness and delicacy unknown on earth that we declared our love.

Later on, after we were married, it often happened that we would travel together in space, with a sweetness of sensation impossible to describe.

When I project my astral body in my bedroom, it is my custom to kiss my wife before going on with my experiments. One day, when I was projected and standing beside her, she said: "Stay near me!"

"Instead, you come with me," I answered.

Immediately freeing herself from her physical body she joined me. We went and sat down on a settee which was placed nearby, and I made her understand the nature of the impressions we can experience in this state. When I kissed her, I pointed out the deluge of sensations which followed. Her love penetrated into my being under the guise of a general warmth, while a feeling of absolute

confidence filled my spirit. On the other hand, my
aura penetrated hers and I had the sensation as if
melting into her. So intense were the vibrations
that I experienced a kind of giddiness. I felt that
if I pushed the experience to its furthest limit the
abnormal speed of the vibrations would make me
lose consciousness.

However, I wished to analyse this experience as
deeply as possible in order to become aware of the
exact degree of spiritual union it is possible to
attain. On this point I received all possible satisfaction.

During one of the experiments I noted the
following facts:

I wished to unite my psychical body with that of
my wife in order to note the physiological and
psychological effects. In the atmosphere in which
we had projected ourselves I could see our more
material doubles united in the form of a cloud.
Heavy at first, it began to clear in proportion to the
greater and greater intimacy with which our subtle
bodies interpenetrated one another. The trans-
parency increased until soon we seemed no more
than a vapour which was hardly visible.

The psychological reactions and sensations of
this state were really extraordinary.

As the cloud became clearer I had the impression
of taking off a series of clothes and becoming more
and more intimately united with my wife. At the
same time I could feel the vibrations of this state
as if I were living in a psychological moment to
which there was no end.

The observations of this rather banal experience
can in no way be compared with those which I have

been able to make in the state of Unity-Multiplicity. In fact, so much as the last described experiment was greater than anything on earth so much are the experiences obtained in a state of Unity-Multiplicity greater than the aforesaid experience.

The realization, something of whose characteristics I have already tried to describe to you, could not have happened without the intermediary help of my wife, with whom my conscious individuality was for a moment united.

Words are powerless to describe the hypersensations of this state of super-consciousness. In no other experience have I had so wideawake a consciousness, no love so powerful, nor a calm and serenity so profound.

It was as if an ocean of love was taking possession of the bed. When the individuality of my wife united with mine, she brought a shade which was hardly perceptible, which then melted into my love, giving it a considerable expansion. The aura, the atmosphere thus generated became myself. By the exercise of the powers attached to this spiritual state, all our faculties are melted into a unity of conscious life. The radiation of consciousness, thus universalized, awakened in every atom of my being a kind of quivering which augmented the delicacy and sweetness of the spiritual harmony in which I found myself immersed.

Each particle of the invisible space was myself in the same way as the sum total of the grains of energy which had awakened in my spherical aura. With remarkable ease I was able to act with equal facility in the whole or in any given fraction of the space thus limited. This was carried out with an intensity of reactive energy proportionate to the action. Reciprocally, all thought, all desire, all consciousness, and all love only form one gentle and serene unity, acting as if from a general impulse from the whole being. Fatigue is non-existent. There is no expenditure of energy. Action manifests in an immense happiness and by a deeper love.

All these conceptions of universal or cosmic consciousness, existing in a unity which lies outside phenomenal time, are very difficult to understand by anyone who has not experienced them. Such difficulty is insignificant, however, compared with the one I am experiencing in trying to describe the extraordinary ease with which, in super-consciousness, we can exercise these almost divine powers.

It is this fact which most surprises me when I think about this extraordinary experience. My physical consciousness asks why it is that so unimaginable a difference exists between the poverty of our earth, the difficulty and clumsiness of our methods of action, and the riches, the harmonies, and prodigious ease with which the universal prerogatives can manifest.

I am still short of the truth when I say that, by analogy, in this supreme state we feel at home with an intimacy, a reality, which has not its equal in any of the other separative states of the ether. However ingrained our terrestrial habits, the ease with which we put them into practice cannot compare with the instinctive manner with which we handle the directives of a whole world.

We now no longer think of the constants of the

past and the future. We "are" purely and simply, in a perfect present which unites in itself all the prerogatives which lie beyond the power of human conception and which human beings have at all times attributed to their gods.

CHAPTER VIII

UNIVERSAL ATTRACTION AND THE PERSONAL EQUATION IN THE HIGHER WORLDS

THE nearer we draw to the limits of our universe in its aspect of pure energy, the more difficult it becomes to express our ideas and observations as these become more generalized.

Also, in this domain, it is necessary to be very circumspect in judging the particular equation of the Higher Being living in the sublimated regions of the universe.

In order to form an accurate judgment it is useful, even indispensable, to have previously penetrated into the various strata of the radio-active ether. We then learn how to notice a delicate shade in the surrounding aura of the Higher Beings. However delicate this may be, it is none the less as real as any other general characteristic.

Before going any further with my remarks on this important subject, I would like you, first of all, to realize the fact that, at this moment, we are analysing "shades of harmony," and it would be sacrilege to say that it is a fault not to find the same characteristics in all beings.

Let us, for example, consider the love of Jesus. This Higher Being, worshipped as a god, is the most easily accessible of our Brothers. On three different occasions have I been able to contact Him in a stratum where His manifestation was possible. It is quite beyond my powers to describe the many thousands of attractions which emanate from such a presence. No word could depict the sensations of well-being, of calm, of peace, and of happiness which all blend in one immense attraction. A rush of love-consciousness caught me up, rushed away with my whole being, and filled me with a limitless sense of confidence. It was no longer necessary for me to think: judgment was both beyond and beneath me; I was able to understand and love all at once, without any veil coming between us, to mar the great comprehension and the immense affection which I experienced.

Were I to analyse the dominant characteristics of such a love I would find there sweetness, simplicity, and goodness.

This in no way means that the other Great Beings are not overflowing with gentleness, goodness, and simplicity, which are part and parcel of the eternal qualities which we must all acquire. But in the harmony of which the love of Jesus is formed, all these qualities are "raised" to their highest pitch.

I would like you to keep in mind this characteristic of exaltation, this dominant note among all the qualities of our attractions. This is the only co-efficient, the fundamental note which is retained by all Beings who have arrived at perfection.

Once evolution has come to an end, various ways open out before the Perfect Being. All possess particular and general characteristics which inter-penetrate in a reciprocal manner, all in an admirable orderliness which is an essential part of the basic harmony of their principles. In this supreme synthesis we may meet a category of Beings to whom I wish to draw your attention. They are the spirits of pure love. Instead of being exalted in only one shade of the harmony their consciousness manages to include all the modalities in a perfect equilibrium. The multiple shades of the chains of harmony which are opened to the Perfect Being, are dissolved into them with a tint hardly different from the eternal principle of life. Their numerical order is comprised in all the others. They are sufficiently distinguishable from the universal consciousness to obviate any mistake being made between them, but their love represents the most general aspect. By analogy, we might compare them to a crystal where each Perfect Being would see his own traits reflected. This pure love with which they are animated welds together all the attracting shades of harmony. It gives without counting the cost, and sees itself only in the infinite varieties of harmony, whose eternal spouse this love must always remain. The works of these Supreme Beings are meant to be used by all the chains of harmony.

During one of my projections I met a young man on a fairly high plane. We fell into conversation on the subject of self-projection and interplanetary journeying. Observing this young man, I was struck by the peace, bliss and serenity of his aura. However, there was one note which dominated all others: an extraordinary calm allied to a characteristic sweetness. If I were to compare the magnetic gentleness of this young man's aura with that of the Jesus consciousness, I would note a difference. The fluidic benevolence of our Eldest Brother is, in some way, more general and universal. That of the young man in question I would describe as being more velvety, more tender.

In the same region as the one above I was approached by an unknown person. As before, I was projected with a supra-lucid realization of my double state. I moved around this person, taking careful note of the radiations which illuminated him on all sides. I cannot remember his appearance and the thoughts we exchanged, but I was so attracted by his auric atmosphere that, had it been possible, I would have liked to stay there for ever. My whole being responded to this tremendous attraction, into which I would have liked to melt my own being. I noticed, however, a limitless devotion which seemed to be an integral part of this great love. In the advanced harmonies which seemed to rise from this love I noticed an incredibly high degree of goodness. When it came to noting my experience, I could only find one word for my note-book: marvellous!

It is evident that gentleness, calm, serenity, and simplicity reign in their highest form in such an atmosphere. However, in this richness of the tones of limitless love I was able to distinguish, by making comparisons with my previous experiences, a special quality of sheer goodness which affected me in a manner quite different from the other cases.

During another experience I found myself walking about, on a high plane, with a Being who took on the appearance of a fair-haired young man. We were exchanging ideas on universal love and specially on the chain of correspondences. I called him my elder brother and embraced him before going away from his wonderful atmosphere. His magnetic aura had the characteristics which are constant in all the higher beings. His magnetic emanations, alternatingly growing and diminishing, gave me a sensation of heat and inexpressible well-being, and, when I embraced him, it was as if I were experiencing a sense of immense love. It seemed as if I were melting with him into one unique love.

In this case, again, I was aware of a factor which was distinct from those I had already noticed in other Beings. This particular harmony was that of brotherly love exalted to an infinite degree.

When we find ourselves among this superabundant richness of tones and these harmonious exaltations of the constants of the universal attraction, it is impossible to manifest any sort of preference. In analysing these masses of sublime vibrations, we are irresistibly attracted towards all the different categories, all the varying shades, with an impetus which is characterized by a unique abandonment of self. It is the particularly exalted characteristics of our own aura which join up with the individual equation (the only term which I can apply to beings who cannot be said to have personalities in our sense of the word) of the Higher Beings and which allow us to discern their qualities.

The recital of these harmonious syntheses of the attraction which becomes individualized in the Higher Beings can give no true conception of their intense reality. In order to appreciate them it is necessary to have lived consciously in the immense freedom of the super-dimensions of space. Our language, moreover, does not possess sufficient qualifying adjectives to express the innumerable variety of shades which can be observed in the Eternal Love.

In order to give you some idea of the manner in which we should conceive these abstractions which sum up the one and only reality of the evolutionary synthesis, let us assume that you could define the different qualities of the universal attraction pertaining to each colour, as well as to their intermediate shades. This process would have to be repeated for the whole scale of tones and their relationship compared with the scale of colours. Then do the same for all the known wave-lengths—and you will find yourself no further advanced than before. All the whirling, intermingling scales of the universal attraction which can be observed in our universe, only represent one note in the infinite multiplicity of universes which are capable of being formed in the womb of eternity.

CHAPTER IX

DESPITE the fact that we are now going to touch on
the borderlines of mysticism I feel that, considering the century in which we are living, it would be
well to define and explain how we can discern
experimentally the fundamental qualities of the
universal energy. This attractive essence which has
an influence on all the forms of energy which are
to be found in the universal matter gives to the man
who can place his consciousness within its orbit a
state of peace which passeth all understanding.

This cosmic consciousness which, for lack of a
better expression, we may classify as divine, has no
connection with our conceptions of good and
evil.

In the existing disorder of our ideas on this subject, in the unleashing of egotistical passions, and
in the social turmoil which is the result, it is usually
impossible to obtain sufficient calmness to make a
proper judgment of the directive energies of the
universal life.

Religion, science, and philosophy quarrel about
extreme qualities, from opposing points of view,
without dreaming for a moment that in order to

obtain a balanced vision a medium must be found which is free from all preconceived ideas.

This is only human. We have all passed through alternatives of extreme opinions, and we always tend to exaggerate the importance of a personal point of view.

I have not the space to give a dissertation on the fundamental Trinity of the Unity. I would rather refer you to the special works on this subject. If you are really desirous of breaking off all attachments to the lower degrees of life, it is essential that you should begin by habituating your consciousness to thinking mathematically, in terms of figures. If you do this you will, little by little, become aware of an order of things free from all the usual attributes which have been added by the human imagination. A new scheme will unfold itself, from which you will be able to understand the role played by the human being in nature.

I am not of the opinion that ideas and beliefs should be broken down brutally and suddenly. However great an element of error these may contain, they are essentially relative to the character, the temperament, the personality of those who hold them, and are therefore necessary. Whatever the ideal which we wish to attain, it is not enough to preconceive a good state; more important is it to give people the means by which they may reach it.

For example: In the state of society to-day, how are we to ally a moral ideal with the need to live in the midst of a taxation which makes living impossible? It is very difficult. There are cases when it becomes impossible to differentiate between honesty and dishonesty. However much he may seem like a good apostle, the moral counsellor dies of indigestion, whilst the idealist famishes.

When we reflect, when we think, and when we reason and meditate on the harmonious fundamentals expressed in these pages, we realize that the balance of our faculties requires that we should not forget that we do have an earthly life. When we contemplate divine love we should always consider it possible that it should be utilized as a means of relieving human suffering.

I would add another piece of good advice. When you find yourself in the midst of an organization, scientific, philosophical, or religious, whose aim is to raise the human race towards some ideal or other, note what part it is willing to play in human suffering. Ask of such a society what it is doing in order to alleviate misfortune; what organizations has it founded in order to bring relief in case of need? Then if all such a society can give you to bite on are theories, beware lest such an organization destroy whatever little material happiness you have by disorganizing all your hopes.

The man or woman who is able to live in the calm state which is needed in order to realize an ideal, who is going to be progressively detached from the ordinary interests and obligations of life, can obtain results which are inestimable. The true union between human consciousness and cosmic consciousness gives the key to the riddle of Good and Evil. The works of such a person will always be balanced, and show tolerance in accordance with the intrinsic quality of beings and things.

All the opinions, all the beliefs, all the experiences through which the human being learns to evaluate the constants of life, when they reach the peak of evolution, melt into a state of supreme, universal love. As we have seen, in this universalized state, each person keeps his or her own personal equation, which permits access to a multiplicity of joys in relationship with the never-ending multitude of regenerated Beings.

Unity-multiplicity, such is the seal of the Absolute, which sanctifies individual perfection. This certainty lies within the reach of every one who has courage and love, without it being necessary for him to weaken this reality by means of imaginary hypotheses. And, though this is the most simple of all states, it cannot be described except by using the most complex forms of analysis.

If we consider the general state of Unity-multiplicity, outside such small variations as are produced by different consciousnesses, the universal attraction that we generally designate under the name of divine love represents that quality of "Unity" which animates all the shades of attraction of human individuality.

With the speed of lightning, the unity of harmony gives us the impression of melting in a love of the world. As if through thousands of channels we find that we can feel, think, cogitate, and conceive with an ease which is nothing short of prodigious. The gentleness, serenity, and calm of this state are wrapped in a peace and fullness of life which is formed from these melted down and unified sensations.

If we make a comparison of these characteristics by means of the earthly consciousness, we notice a particular impulse made up of a blend of confidence and abandon. Without quite experiencing a feeling of unworthiness, this consciousness becomes prey to a state of deep dissatisfaction, due to the momentary clairvoyance in which it sees all it might have done. All matters of personal interest, all cravings for joy, for peace, even for happiness, no longer interfere with the steady flow of pure consciousness. However noble and disinterested it might be, all ambition disappears. The earthly consciousness is now capable of undertaking the greatest possible sacrifices in order to balance up the wave of love which it is receiving. In the presence of this immense onrush of universal love which saturates it, the personality of the individual knows and understands, without the least doubt, that it will always be a debtor whatever the efforts it makes. It is fully conscious of the fact that even the most extreme sacrifices which it might accomplish, the most intense pains it could endure, would not come up to the same level as the millionth part of the fundamental qualities of this ocean of harmony from which such benefits are being obtained.

Apart from the personal equation, I do not think that it is possible to analyse the extraordinary richness of the harmonious tones which reveal themselves under the influence of this unity. The very intensity of the wave of reactive energy which lifts up the consciousness into the ability to express, practically, such an attraction is beyond the range of metaphor. We are now outside the limits of our universe and any form of expression serves only to weaken the relationship which I am trying to express.

This super-devotion, this conscious super-sacrifice which invades the personality of the thinker who is

making contact with his "Unity I," might be translated as the emission of a wave of joy, fully conscious
and infinitely gentle, infinitely happy, infinitely
sweet and serene.   It would seem as if this wave of
super-being meets another wave coming from outside which penetrates its most intimate atoms.

The fecundation of this personal wave of energy
by means of the ocean of cosmic radiations, brings to
birth sensations which are of a delicacy and sweetness unimaginable.   The contact between these
personal and cosmic spheres of energy is at one
time a unity and a multiplicity—a unity through the
absolute synthesis of all the personal elements which
group together in a similar abandon towards the
centre, towards the origin of all life and cosmic love.

The multiple element comes in owing to the flood
of feeling and awareness which is brought to birth
at the same instant.   Once again unity, owing to
the expansive sweetness and bliss which is communicated to all the atoms of the consciousness.

A multiplicity owing to the wave of creative
desires which it engenders.

A unity owing to the supreme happiness of being
and feeling ourselves loved with such a divine
intensity.

A multiplicity owing to the waves of affection of
varying shades which flow from us.

From the physiological point of view the human
body is influenced by this spiritual communion.
An infinite sense of sweetness and bliss fills every
fibre.   Tears flow naturally.   This communion is so
essentially sweet and pure that we have the feeling
of all the centres of life being merged gently into a
deep peace.

In order to make an exact analysis of this communion between the human being and his origin, this state should never be evoked by auto-suggestion.

Meditation and contemplation will help us to tune in to its vibrations. In its finest state this union must occur spontaneously, must be a sudden illumination of the earthly consciousness.

To endeavour to put down all the details of the mysterious Flame of such a conjunction is to try to express the inexpressible. All the same, it does not seem out of place, during a century when people are saying so many insignificant things, when so many absurdities are written, that someone should express once and for all, some tangible, real, and eternal truths.

The details which have been given at different times by unbalanced minds which wished to deal with this question of the regeneration of the individual consciousness in the cosmic consciousness, without having themselves made the necessary efforts, does not prove anything against a truth and reality of which certain proof is obtainable by anyone willing to make the necessary efforts.

In the spiritual essence which springs forth from such a communion, we become aware of the fact that a union takes place between the source and the outlet of all forms of universal attraction. This contact gives us the impression of eternal youth, of an eternal splendour in the eternal present of a love without end.

We are made aware of an instantaneous evolution, without beginning or end, in a unity which is the germ of all past and future evolution.

Whatever may be its range of expansion or contraction, this immense love remains itself without either size or duration. It is the point whose circumference is everywhere and whose centre is nowhere. It is the origin of all forms of universal energy, it is the infinite synthesis of all spiritual potentials, it is the Finite coming into equilibrium with the Infinite in an eternal Present.

CHAPTER X

THE negative tendencies of experimental science gives any charlatan an exceptional power to exploit the credulity of the public.

It is for these reasons that I insist on the need of personal work if we wish to arrive at any results of permanent worth. Start by realizing that magical powers have no existence. No one can give you a lasting power unless you have developed it for yourself.

I have now made my point of view quite clear. This done I propose giving you the following hints which may help you both to develop and to control your results. We have already seen (Part I, Chapter XVI) that inspiration is in no way related to the supernatural atmosphere with which it is usually surrounded. It is a method of working which becomes a habit by practice.

The method of reflection in which we contact the first rudiments of this faculty is called "meditation."

The rational exercise of meditation must be put into practice, as I have already pointed out, by the

225

concentration of the mind on the essential elements
of any question, as if we were in complete ignorance
of its nature, and seek to find a solution to something quite strange to us. Meditation is not a
reverie, a blank gaze lost in the depths of infinity,
but the putting into action of a sustained, voluntary
and conscious attention. The logical processes
of analysis and synthesis used in this way
give remarkable results. Precision, clarity of
thinking, and common sense are indispensable
if we wish to maintain a good balance between
our faculties and develop them on the higher
planes.

The observations carried out during self-projection
are a great help to the practice of meditation, and
allow it to work in a field where its possibilities are
greatly increased.

With the practice of this method of rational
meditation the consciousness becomes familiar with
a new order of vibrations, and the inspiration which
springs from this becomes, through habit, a normal
faculty.

What we know as contemplation is far less well
understood. It is, however, a natural sequel to
meditation. To consider contemplation as beatific
adoration, more or less unconscious, is an error for
which we can easily forgive those who have not
made a study of the subject. Contemplation is not
a blind, suggestive repetition of words, desires,
feelings, or prayers.

On the contrary, this mental exercise exacts the
strictest training, and one which must always be
definitely rational. I repeat: the more we draw
near to the initial relationship which exists in the

system of Cause and Effect in which we are living and evolving, the more imagination must give way to a far more concentrated form of reasoning, to a more unshakable will, to a greater self-mastery.

Whilst it is within the reach of all to create an imaginary heaven and to endow it with all the attributes we may wish, it is necessary, on the other hand, to be an Initiate; that is to say, absolute master of meditation and of self-projection in the higher planes, in order that consciousness may be able to appreciate the constants of harmony in their true simplicity.

The practice of contemplation must not be an intellectual reverie, but the continuation and stabilization of the exercises of meditation, and the fixation of the ideas obtained by inspiration.

This complementary exercise is usually practised lying down on a comfortable couch, in a state of relaxation, which produces a stillness, and a removal of all nervous tension. The next step is to make a clear, lucid and absolutely conscious exposition of the motives which inspire you, and the reasons which induce you to love a principle whose keynote is harmony.

We start off by considering a cause which will bring about effects of which we are aware. The scale of these causes is very extensive. It begins with the general effects which we are used to observing, rising progressively until it reaches the directive principles of evolution.

Now it will be quite easy for you to realize that there is nothing mysterious in the practice of contemplation. Its aim is to fix in the consciousness the impulses and states which it has reached. It would be an exaggeration to make it into the basis for a mystical system. All the criticisms which are aimed at contemplation only serve to show the lack of organization in methods of psychic development. When alternated with the practice of meditation, contemplation allows the individuality to become fully aware of what it is doing. Never must it be allowed to lapse into sentimental day-dreaming, for the mere pleasure of experiencing new sensations. This practice should keep the attention fixed on the laws of the universe, then on the directing principles of evolution. In this way it opens out canals for the energy of the higher worlds. It accelerates tremendously the results of meditation, and opens the way to inspiration.

To sum up, remember that the practice of contemplation requires as its basis: The consciousness of the effect whose cause is being contemplated, the consciousness of the cause whose basic principle is being contemplated, the consciousness of the principle whose spiritual essence is being contemplated.

As the higher consciousness rises into this hierarchy the reaction develops in the lower consciousness a stability, a fixity of purpose, and a calm which makes it independent of the results of its actions. Eventually this road ends in the bringing together of the individual and the universal by a meeting between these two systems of energy. Infinite smallness now unites itself with infinite greatness. The regenerated human being becomes conscious of the immense solidity which ties him, on one side to the vibrant unity to which he owes his life, and on the other to the multiplicity through which this energy expresses itself. This occurrence is the opportunity for man to realize many different forms of bliss.

PART III
CONCLUSIONS

CHAPTER I

THE CERTAINTY OF DELIVERANCE FROM EVIL

IT is only when we stand face to face with actual experience, the reality of which takes possession of the whole being, reducing his previous beliefs to nothing, that we realize the hardihood of those pioneers of humanity who came to these same conclusions by undergoing the same experiences.

Formerly the dogma of survival has been imposed upon the masses; but to prove this truth by striking experiments, is, I feel, the finest method of convincing the multitude.

Unfortunately human consciousness does not evolve by faith alone, but needs especially the development of its intellectual and moral faculties. To impose dogmatic beliefs is to sow the seeds of discord and of fratricidal wars.

Scientific progress has rendered real services to these studies. In spreading the knowledge of the universal law of Cause and Effect which rules phenomenal existence, it has done more towards helping human relationships and making people more tolerant, than all the philosophic dissertations.

As we know that the same causes bring about the same effects, if we put them into action in the same circumstances, opinions and beliefs must change in value. "Either we know or we do not know." In the latter case it is wiser to keep silent unless we wish to give others the opportunity of making ironic remarks which are fairly well founded.

After all, why should we repeat obstinately, like parrots, ideas which we have adopted by chance, coincidence, instinctive affinity or hereditary suggestion?

Scientific philosophers are working on a sound basis when they maintain that we are unconsciously influenced by associations of ideas provoked by custom, environment, education, heredity, the historical past, and so on.

Everything, or almost everything, has been said about the majority of questions upon which we build up our theories. Many of the ideas which are considered as new, are nothing but whited sepulchres. In order to escape from routine and prejudice in order to have individualized, original ideas, it is necessary to form the habit of reasoning and thinking. It is excellent training to meditate on the laws of life and to draw from these conclusions which are in agreement with the order of nature; providing we do not allow ourselves to be influenced by academic doctrines which are often a hindrance to freedom of judgment.

In order to bring back some balance into the disarray of our modern theories, a new fact was needed. This fact, like every other, must submit of the law of Cause and Effect. Furthermore, everyone must be capable of proving this fact by the same experiments repeated in equivalent circumstances.

It is from this standpoint that I have analysed some of the characteristics of conscious self-projection. To separate ourselves into two distinct parts, one of which will be standing a few yards away from the other, which lies inert but living, to have full mastery over our conscious and sensory faculties, is an all-embracing certainty. It is also a source of new ideas. It is a mine of knowledge. It is the starting-point of a greater, wider and more complete life. It is the end of all our sorrows, of all worry concerning the painful enigma of survival.

At any rate, now that we know, we can commence to live in a real sense of the word. Up to the present you have probably, like the majority of humanity, been tossed from shore to shore of the river of doubt by the opinions and beliefs, sometimes satisfied, sometimes deceived, passing through alternations of joy and despair. What pain, what suffering, have we not been forced to endure owing to this fatal ignorance concerning the fact of survival! What fears have been born of this same ignorance! Beneath the vainglorious domination of the powers that be, man has been forced to bow his trembling frame beneath the perpetual menace of vengeful deities. At each step, fathomless pits have opened beneath his feet. Every day it has seemed as if that great arsenal known as "*rights and duties*" took on greater importance. Confusion and anxiety are the inevitable end of such an unstable morality.

Is it true that all that has now disappeared? What is the benevolent energy whose magic wand will allow us to make a clean sweep of all these misfortunes?

Despite everything, we must admit that these new ideas may inspire fear when first we contemplate them. Will they not be blown away by the first breath of rational thinking? Misled, deceived, buffeted by fate, ridiculed for so many centuries, can we be sure that this is not anything but a mirage? The torrent of hope which rises from the depths of our consciousness no longer dares to manifest. It is difficult for anyone to put aside the mask of scepticism when faced by popular irony. How dare we admit this great hope which we sense is being born within us?

This intuition which grips us, this urge of our innermost self, is it no more than a neurosis? Who can tell where mental disorder begins?

It is therefore with circumspection that, timidly at first, we begin to change the normal course of our life in favour of one which is possible outside the limits of our earthly system. Yet, little by little, we begin to become familiar with it. The radiant atmosphere which is brought about by the practical manifestation of these ideas is so sweet that one would be a fool to neglect it. We fall into the habit of living this new life. The anxieties of life become annihilated before the light which begins to manifest within us. Soon we find that we are no more so interested in ordinary material pleasures. Far deeper forms of satisfaction are born within us.

Life is no longer a quicksand. Every day we find that we are treading with a firmer step. Soon our knowledge will form a rock upon which we shall build the basis of an immortality which shall conquer space.

CHAPTER II

THE CERTAINTY OF A LASTING HAPPINESS

WHEN we consider the period of time during which humanity has been forced to live in an agony of doubt, the conscious certainty of being able to create a happiness which will last, irrespective of the passing phases of life, is a priceless boon.

The word "happiness" is one which bears innumerable meanings. Every one has a different interpretation of it, and quite rightly. Why should anyone impose a certain definite form of happiness on another? The happiness experienced from having eaten when hungry is as respectable as that of having discovered a new scientific law. There are joys, great and small, ephemeral and eternal, illusory and real. There are the joys which neutralize, and joys which complete one another. Is that a reason why we should exalt some at the cost of others? I do not think so. Each one of us must find out, by experience, the happiness which suits him. I submit that it is by becoming aware of the ephemeral nature of the happiness of the senses, and the joys of material life, that the sage identifies himself with the fundamental principles of the universal life.

We should remember that a period of apprentice-ship exists in all things. That of life is variable. Earnest and over-conscientious natures will want to drain the cup of bitterness to its dregs. Soft and docile natures will try to avoid pain by every means. The reasonable and conscientious being who always seeks logical and experimental truth, will neither wish for an intensification nor diminution of his suffering, but rather will profit by whatever experience falls to his lot, and deal with life accordingly.

It is this category of thinkers that I have in mind when writing of happiness which will last eternally.

All the expressions which we can use in order to define happiness are of value only in relation to experience. If we bring into action our new experimental knowledge, happiness is seen to be the normal state of balance of all beings, whatever their degree of evolution.

Every being who follows his natural tendencies cannot be held responsible for a state of affairs which he did not create. The savage who eats his parents in order to honour them with a tomb, cannot be subject to the same kinds of suffering which would grip the conscience of a more developed being.

Good and evil develop in accordance with the expansion of consciousness. What we loosely term good simply sums up the characteristics of a normal development. Evil is a lack of balance, a disorder which exists between the progress of individual faculties and their application.

It is of no avail to discuss the relative value of the

happiness of two beings, one of whom is placed at the highest rung of the evolutionary ladder and the other on the lowest. All we can say is that as soon as there is a balance between the qualities of our being and their application there is Peace.

Pain and suffering are born of discord. This becomes clear in the lives of disincarnate beings living in the nether world. Every one is happy so long as he is not aware of a more developed state. Immediately light is cast upon the substance in which they are living, a comparison is established. Suffering is born. As long as these disincarnate beings have not broken the fetters which hold them prisoners in the lower worlds, their remorse will become greater as they consider their past misdeeds.

The pain of not being able to satisfy a life which is wider, more complete, more in agreement with our real selves, gives ample proof of its necessity. All the expressions by means of which we idealize our intuitive desires are only of value in relation to the state of consciousness with which they correspond. It is useless to try to give some one sensations and impressions which are the fruit of a state of consciousness which he has never experienced. Logic and reason require that we give the consciousness a means of realizing a higher degree of understanding in the hierarchy of causes and principles, in order that it may experience the corresponding happiness.

By means of experience, which is the product of experiment, it becomes easy to see the influence wielded by collective ideas on the development of happiness. All procedures whose aim lies in dogmatizing ideas, feelings or facts, upon a pre-established order of things, hinder the growth of happiness.

All those organizations which have as their aim the establishment of a lasting peace, of a greater social balance, of a more rational organization, must tend towards greater freedom of thought.

In giving to all the necessary instruction for forming a free judgment, more is done for the happiness of a people than by nourishing them on dogmas and paradoxes.

There is an enormous difference between a free judgment, and one that is false. The former brings about repercussions on its author which he will himself rectify when he understands the painful reaction. The latter brings about a crystallization, a general inability to put into action the necessary efforts to establish a balance more in agreement with our mental evolution.

It is thus quite useless to discuss the priority of any procedure, or special method of finding happiness. All those means which start by calling on logical reasoning are good, so long as we do not become obstinate over ideas which we do not understand.

The method of meditation, or reflection, which splits up ideas into their elementary principles, in order to reconstruct them, is one of the most efficacious means for everybody.

The Higher Life possesses some elements whose

certainty lies beyond all doubt. Evolution is the easiest possible idea to conceive. It is a natural sequence in the development of the consciousness, towards which we are led by an observation of the facts of our daily life.

CHAPTER III

WHEN we examine the life of the people around us
we note the poverty of effort directed towards self-
perfection. The majority of people allow themselves
to be guided by their appetites, and by the ties of
specific and general events in the social life. Few
dare to try to swim upstream in order to create for
their personal use circumstances more in accord
with a better life.

The conditions of life in the invisible teach us
that nature is a great store-house of energy into
which the human being has but to delve in order to
bring to light faculties well beyond the ordinary
development.

So long as the individual does not take himself in
hand he is a slave to the particular and general
reactions of the events in which he is living. The
law of equilibrium is not concerned with
suffering. Under a multitude of forms each one
can discover the qualities which he must develop in
order to master those conditions which are unfavour-
able to his existence.

The first principle of this organization, of this
personal reform, is "confidence." Whatever may

be the difficulties of life we must never lose courage and must keep an unshakable confidence in its laws. We must realize that harmony, equilibrium and order compose the universe even to its most minute fractions. If, in our personal life, we put the same elements into action, we must inevitably arrive at results which are more in conformity with our desires.

As moral suffering is the result of a lack of balance between our desires, our thoughts, our feelings and our social obligations, all we have to do in order to make it disappear is to organize and bring into line our affections and tendencies. Following upon the same way of thinking the physiological organism has to undergo a more severe discipline and therefore disease cannot overcome us so easily.

The second principle of a harmonious life is "goodwill." Now that we have firmly established in ourselves confidence in the laws of life, we have no reason for wishing ill to those who are less advanced than we. Let us leave it to quarrelsome, argumentative and suspicious minds to create their own complications in life. After all they are working for themselves. So far as egotism, pride and vanity are concerned, these faults are so widespread that it would be in vain to try to eliminate them from our surroundings. Goodwill shields us from evil tc gues, protects us from envy, gives us strength to bear with the thousands of faults which we see around us.

The third condition of success is to think unceasingly of the results to be obtained. Man is essentially a thinking being. The association between those images which we call ideas, has no limits. So soon as we step across the successive dimensions of the plane in which we live, these ideas become unified with the very principle of energy whose realized forms they represent.

In order to obtain powerful results, thoughts of goodwill must be guided. Thought is a force which has to be directed consciously, with good sense and logic. It would be a mistake to think that it is necessary to lead a special kind of life in order to obtain results.

The ancient initiations, occult tests, and magical spells, were all adapted to states of consciousness which could not have developed by any other means. The most trivial facts in our lives can serve as rungs in the development of our powers and faculties. In his own particular sphere of action each one of us can progress as easily as in the temples of Memphis. All that is needed is to concentrate on one purpose the entire sum of one's thoughts and desires. In the case with which we are concerned, this purpose must be that of progress and evolution. We must consider all events, whether good or evil, as lessons from which to draw useful conclusions concerning the path we are treading.

If our social condition does not help us with the work we wish to accomplish, let us be patient and seek to achieve the best we may. Inevitably things will improve. We may have difficulties in our family or social surroundings; never mind, let us stand firm in our goodwill. A few appropriate home truths will eliminate the greater, or lesser, asses who are circulating around us. Human stupidity is a mine of "awful examples" which we shall learn to use for our own improvement.

The habit of seeing the smallest details of life as a means of drawing deductions useful to our development, brings out qualities of observation which will increase, and bring about the birth of new faculties. It is for each to use the faculties in the manner which best suits him. Whatever they may be, now and always they lead to the same goal of perfection.

There is a very simple way of finding out if we are taking the wrong road. We have seen that attraction is the universal principle which brings human and cosmic energy together. Multiple in the lower strata of the universal substance, all forms of attraction unite in the higher states to become a concurrent Unity-Multiplicity functioning in the Perfect Being.

If this work of reorganization has been carried out well, we shall become aware of an attraction of the Being drawing all things towards a collective good. This attractive tendency is surrounded by an aura of quietness and peace. As it develops and strengthens, the personal interest is transformed into a joyous interest, then into love of the directing influences of the Good, the Beautiful, and True. This goes on until the human being becomes consciously identified with a universal love which includes all beings and all things.

CHAPTER IV

CONCERNING CERTAINTIES AND PROBABILITIES

ALTHOUGH I have done my best to avoid the use of ambiguous terms, it is far from an easy task to give an exact definition of the forces functioning in the universe. Nevertheless, it is of use to schematize their action, generally, in order to prepare the consciousness for their experimental realization.

If we visualize the mechanism of this organization, we can say that self-projection opens the door for strict experimentation in a new field of activity.

With its aid all metaphysical phenomena may be studied scientifically. The transformation of energies may be directly controlled. All the manifestations of the living and the dead become new subjects for inquiry. All forms, all modes of thought may be studied, as it were, on the spot.

For this purpose three operators are needed. The first is the one who projects himself from the physical body, in order to decide on and prepare for various physical or psychical experiments. The second operator mesmerizes a subject who is charged with passing on useful comments and observations.

This direct control in the dimensions where the phenomena occur will prove of great service. The composition of the atom, the constitution of the various bodies, the inter-blending and disintegration of the grains of energy, are all going to open out new vistas on the origin of the universal substance.

These analyses will allow us to go far more intimately into the mysteries of life. The action of different medicines, studied from this point of view, gives precious information with regard to the healing of disease. The Elixir of life, the Philosopher's Stone, will now become realities. The principle of self-projection is within the range of science. In the present work I stress the need for a psychological and moral development because I foresee the possibility that the student will be able to penetrate into other worlds, and wish him to do this with the least inconvenience. Apart from that, to use a new kind of energy without any moral development would increase disorder and prove dangerous to all concerned. But, from the phenomenal point of view, there is no doubt that the physiological mechanism of self-projection can be brought down to a scientific technique. In this case, so long as he knows all the needs of his own particular temperament, there is no reason why anyone should not be able to project himself.

Thus we can well imagine, in the future, an adept ordering his patient or pupil a special regimen in order to modify his radio-active potential. This latter will only have to place himself in a room ionized by colours, perfumes and radiations suitable to a favourable atmosphere for automatic self-projection.

There is no doubt concerning the part of self-projection. It is manifest to the most sceptical. To suppose that I have been able to imagine all the details of the experiences I have related would be to endow me with qualities far more perfect than those needed in order to project the astral body.

A second certainty is impressed on all who come into touch with the invisible worlds. It is the certainty of the evolution of consciousness, with which is associated the highest imaginable bliss. This certainly includes all others. It is therefore of paramount importance that it should be acquired. Step by step I have myself experienced its many variations. I have explored tentatively and gropingly the successive states of consciousness one after the other, and have come, finally, to a total immersion in Cosmic Consciousness.

I can therefore fearlessly affirm that evolution is the general law of every living being. I have already cited certain characteristics observed on the spot: infinite bliss, absolute freedom and well-being. Perfect love, at once individual and universal. Unity of consciousness; multiplicity of powers. From these truths come many others. For instance: that death is an illusion. The supremacy of Good, of Order, in all degrees of evolution. The certainty of immortality in an eternal present. The non-existence of time and space; and many more which it would be puerile to enumerate.

Then what is now left for us to know? Perhaps details concerning weight and measurement. The intimate nature of energy and substance. We could also draw lines of demarcation between the different states of space, their number, their size, their possibilities, the means of interpenetration. We might also study the nature of the projected double and of consciousness. These are all questions about which we have little data. But these are of secondary importance since we have the means of studying them.

I think that in all things it is the result which must be considered. The essential need is not to argue to infinity, but rather to understand the relationships which unite us to nature, to the laws of life, of equilibrium, of the fundamental principles of the universal order. Definitions are only of value in relation to our understanding of these correspondences. Once the individuality has attained full consciousness, of what import is the relativity of words! It knows quite well that it can reproduce the same phenomena, at any moment, by bringing into play the laws and relations of which it is conscious.

All questions of certainty rest on a progressive awareness of Fundamental Causes and Principles. So far as definitions are concerned, these are infinite, as they are adapted to the degree of evolution which a being may have attained.

Let us take an example. The certainty of my observations in the different degrees of the ether allows me to visualize the schematic constitution of the universe, without having a thorough knowledge of the intimate nature of the universal substance. Whatever hypotheses I may form, the whole remains true, because I would always try to adapt my earthly knowledge to the process that I have observed.

In order to fix our ideas, let us consider a virgin substance, an impalpable ether, whose grains of energy are in an indifferent equilibrium, outside all forms of pressure going in any direction. Whether the atoms are separated by one metre or one kilometre, it is of no consequence. This is infinity, in which time and space do not exist.

Let us suppose that, by the power of thought, I produce a pressure. Whatever may be the direction of this attraction I immediately create a limitation. The intensity of the centripetal force will be proportionate to my act, which will have determined the idea of duration, of space, and of matter. As soon as I refrain from action, the atoms, returning to their normal state, bring about the idea of a centrifugal force. The material aspect is now transformed and is replaced by quality: force.

Again, we can imagine a pendulum which pushes back the universal substance to a maximum point of compression and returns to its point of departure minus a fraction of interest. Let an impulse return this interest (used by the resistance of the surrounding atmosphere) each time, and the scientific notions on potential energy and the energy of movement are enough to maintain the stability of the universe. As to the relationship existing between the point of suspension and the extremity of the pendulum this will represent the constant relationship between that which is absolute and that which is relative. Whatever may be the size of a circle, or a sphere, every one knows that the relationship between circumference and diameter is invariable.

The conceptions of equilibrium at each point of space can also be worked out easily in a schematic way. Let us assume that the quantity of substance in a universe be equal to one hundred units. We could consider the extremity known as crude matter as being made up of ninety-nine parts of crude matter and one part of pure energy. Reciprocally, we shall have ninety-nine parts of pure energy and one part of crude matter at the opposite extremity. Now, in all the fractions of this imaginary universe we shall always have one hundred units with a variable proportion in the aspects pure energy and crude matter. From which we have our conceptions of constant equilibrium and of the transformation of energy.

In whatever degree these hypotheses may be illusory, I shall always finish up at the essential points of experience.

(1) One substance, eternal, manifesting under the aspects of matter and force.

(2) A constant equilibrium on every plane.

(3) An energy pressing the atoms towards a centre: crude matter.

(4) Complete absence of pressure: pure force.

(5) The possibility for the human soul to penetrate into each of these states of the universal substance—that which seems heavy and dark, being the crude matter aspect, and that which seems light and luminous being the pure energy aspect.

(6) Lastly, a unity of conscious sensations, which considers the crude matter aspect as an imprisonment of all the faculties with a minimum of satisfaction, and the pure energy aspect as an absolute freedom of action with a maximum of satisfaction.

Do not trouble too much about the definitions which are given in course of this book. Rather try to seize hold of the relationships which are born from them. At each step you take in this path you will understand better why and in what way consciousness is a unity of life capable of expressing itself in a multiplicity of forms.

Do not worry whether humanity will follow you in your deductions. These studies have this about them, that in working for yourself you will open a new field of experience for others. You therefore contribute your share in giving a little more peace to the world. Let every one do as much and evolution will no longer be a mere word.

THE END

CPSIA information can be obtained
at www.ICGtesting.com
Printed in the USA
LVHW061557171219
640805LV00030B/666/P

9 781169 302105